IRISH
GHOSTS

IRISH GHOSTS

Compiled by J. AENEAS CORCORAN

GEDDES & GROSSET

Published 2002 by Geddes and Grosset,
David Dale House, New Lanark, ML11 9DJ, Scotland

© 2002 Geddes and Grosset

ISBN 1 84205 205 5

Printed and bound in Europe

CONTENTS

HAUNTED CHURCHES AND CHURCHYARDS

HAUNTED ISLANDS

POLTERGEISTS

REVENANTS

THE 'TAKEN'

APPENDIX – GHOST VERSES

INTRODUCTION

Fairies and Phantoms

Ireland's fame as a land of fairies and other 'little people' is great. Not only in a host of well-remembered stories and legends, but also in a vast number of actual sites – 'fairy raths', fairy hills, and suchlike – the memory of an earlier, vanished race is preserved and, on the whole, respected. To some observers, it has seemed that the richness of the fairy tradition has eclipsed any claim Ireland has to be a land where other supernatural elements might also exist. Instead of ghosts, they say, Ireland has fairies. In fact, this is not at all true. In a country which has maintained through the centuries a spiritual awareness that was quite a normal attribute of the old Celtic society, together with an abiding sense that the here-and-now is not necessarily the only genuine present, it would be extremely surprising if there were no hint of sensitivity to the paranormal. But of course there is a great deal. Furthermore, fairies are one thing, and an absorbing field of study in their own right; ghosts are something else. Whilst often it seems from the accounts of fairy activity that they work in a similar fashion, there is a basic difference.

It is plain from every account of fairy activity ever written that they are not human; not in possession of human souls. Ghosts, however, it would seem, are very frequently, if not always, the spirits of departed human beings which for various reasons remain attached to a particular location. It is not part of the purpose of this book to explore the causes of this, which seem to range widely, though it appears true to say that some form of psychic disturbance often lies at the base of it. Guilt, violence, unfinished business of one sort or another – these are some of the invisible strings that keep a spirit earthbound when its natural place is elsewhere. But some spirits seem to remain merely because of their great and perhaps excessive attachment to a place or to a family and not through any traumatic event.

The Irish, just like everyone else, are liable to these disturbances, or attachments, and consequently Ireland, just like everywhere else, has its quota of ghosts. From some of the stories in this book it will also be clear that there are other creatures, which cannot be classed as fairies nor as the disturbed and still earthbound spirits of human beings. There is still a great deal that requires methodical investigation.

Banshees

It nevertheless seems true that the worlds of ghosts and fairies overlap. This may be because certain beings which have come to be known as fairies, can discern, and have some power over, the human soul. There is also the case of the banshee, literally 'fairy-woman', a phenomenon restricted, if not to Ireland, then certainly to the Irish (since it has been recorded as heard by Irish people in other parts of the globe). This harbinger of imminent death has a long history, which has been carefully examined by Patricia Lysaght in her book *The Banshee*. The unseen universe beyond our own, which can only be dimly perceived even by those who have some ability to sense it and communicate with it, contains beings which can present themselves in a variety of different ways.

Clergymen

One of the curious aspects of Irish ghost lore is that a large amount of it has been researched, and indeed experienced, by clergymen of the Church of Ireland. The interest taken in occult matters by these Protestant ministers is far greater than that shown by their Catholic colleagues. Indeed, one of the prime source books was compiled by the Reverend John Seymour, a Tipperary rector, and first published in 1914. He already had a book entitled *Irish Witchcraft and Demonology* to his credit. It may be that the Church of Ireland clergymen were more independent-minded. They also very often had less work to do and larger incomes to indulge their interests than the unestablished Catholic priests. However, Seymour does note, a little wryly, that Irish ghosts seemed more responsive to exorcisms carried out by Catholic priests than to those of the Church of Ireland incumbents.

Other Ghost-Researchers

Interest in the occult side of Irish life began to grow rapidly in the 1880s, as 'orders' were formed with the aim of studying and getting closer to the non-physical world. A number of writers were prominent in these inquries, including George Russell (AE) and W. B. Yeats. Another was Yeats's friend and patron, Lady Gregory, whose *Kiltartan Notebooks* contain many first-hand accounts of the occult. The 'ghost-hunter' Elliott O'Donnell was Irish born and bred, though he conducted most of his hunting in other countries. His American counterpart, Hans Holzer, also paid some visits to Ireland and explored a number of haunted locations.

The Animal Tradition

Animals play a large part in many accounts of super-natural events throughout the world, and not least in Ireland. Like some other aspects of the occult, this can be traced far back into Celtic lore, which is rich in stories of shape-shifters: of men who become dogs and dogs that become men; of creatures half-animal and half-human. In one or two of the stories recorded in this book, men put on animal masks in order to carry out evil deeds. It is intriguing in more recent times how frequently tamed animals, such as the domestic cat and dog, and the horse, feature in super-natural appearances, almost as if our own human guilt at stealing their primeval innocence was coming back to accuse us.

Location

The pervasiveness of the supernormal in Ireland is interesting. That traditional location, the old church-yard, is well-represented, and so, as one might expect, is the fairy rath, or fort. But unseen presences have been felt in rural cottages and suburban houses as well as in ancient castles, on lonely Skellig Michael and in the wild Bog of Allen as well as in busy towns and cities. Police stations, schools, and locomotive sheds have been found to house spirits of various kinds, and even the cultivated fields of the country-side, as the account (on page 153) of 'The Thing on the Bicycle' shows, hold their mysteries.

Ireland, then, is most certainly a land of ghosts as well as of fairies. Wherever you are in Ireland – inland, on the coast, on offshore islands or on a Dublin street – it seems that there is more going on than your eyes can see.

ANIMAL SPIRITS

The Speckled Dog

There are many accounts of supernatural beasts in Ireland, with monsters among them, but often they take the form of more familiar creatures, like dogs

Most frequently it is a black dog, but one of Lady Gregory's informants told her of a speckled dog he saw in a house near Loughrea. He had been sent to collect a pig for the butcher and, arriving late, was given a bed for the night. He awoke and looked out, to see a cow in the field eating the potatoes. Going down to drive off the cow, he came into the kitchen where a speckled dog, with spots of black and white and yellow, lay by the hearth. The moment he entered, the dog rose and went out through the door, though the door was both shut and locked.

When he told this to the owners of the house, they were frightened, and begged him to stay another night. That night as he lay in bed, he felt the bedclothes being peeled off, and a heavy blow struck him in the chest, as cold as ice. Terrified, he pulled the bedclothes up again, and covered his head. He left the house next morning, and never returned.

The Spotted Dog

The writer and ghost-hunter Elliott O'Donnell experienced one of those spirits in canine form when he was on a walking-tour in the Irish countryside and obtained a bed for the night in a small cottage kept by a widow. In the course of the night, he was woken by a weird wailing cry, and, sitting up, he saw the form of a large dog, pale in colour, but covered in dark blotchy spots. It opened its mouth to show a great, yellow jaw. Then, abruptly, it vanished, and at the same time he heard again the wailing cry.

In the morning, he questioned the widow, and she told him that although she had often had the feeling there was something uncanny about the place, she had never seen anything. But one of her children had – her son Michael, a sailor who had drowned at sea about a year before. He had slept in the same room as O'Donnell, and often used to see the dog.

'A big, spotted creature, like what we call a plum-pudding dog,' said his mother. 'It was a nasty, unwholesome thing, he used to tell me, and would run round and round his room at night. Though a bold enough lad as a rule, the thing always scared him, and he used to come and tell me about it, with a face as white as linen. He would sometimes throw a boot at it, and always with the same result – the boot would go right through it.'

The woman then told O'Donnell that a former tenant of the house was reputed to have been a witch, and that she had died in that same room.

'Of course,' the woman said, 'it couldn't have been her ghost that Mike saw.'

But O'Donnell was not so sure.

The Black Dog: 1

Many districts of Ireland have tales of a spectral black dog which appears, sometimes on its own, sometimes with the ghost of a person in attendance. Once upon a time, in pagan days, as the Reverend John Seymour suggests, the black dog may have been a river spirit. It has been seen in daytime and at night, both inside houses and in the open air.

One account related to Seymour was from a fellow-clergyman. This man's father, also a clergyman, had kept a farm as well, and one day Seymour's informant, as a boy, heard a day-labourer talk about 'having seen the Devil'. The labourer had been walking along a country road, when at the gate which led in towards a house, he saw a dog. He took it to be a black retriever and thought no more about it, until all of a sudden he found the dog padding silently by his side. He observed that the creature's eyes were blood-red. He picked up some stones to throw at it, but it ignored them, though it presently vanished.

A long time later, the house in question was bought by people known to Seymour's informant. The clergyman was a constant visitor to the house, and was soon aware that the owners were troubled by the appearances of a black dog; and he remembered the experience recounted by the day-labourer, long ago, at the same place. The avenue to the house was a long one, and the dog often appeared beside visitors walking up it, though he himself never witnessed the animal. Although the dog was never known to molest anyone, its sudden appearances were so unnerving and inexplicable that the new owners soon sold up and went elsewhere.

The Black Dog: 2

Another detailed account was given by a lady with a childhood memory from time spent visiting her uncle's large farmhouse in County Tyrone. Aged about ten, she was given a bedroom at the end of a long passage:

'One night I had the most vivid and terrible nightmare – if it was a nightmare! – that I have ever had in my life. I remember it as clearly as if it had only happened last night. I thought I woke and saw a huge curly black dog standing in the room and looking at me. Then he came over to the bed with his mouth open, and his great red tongue hanging out. He snuffed me, and licked my hands and face; after which I saw him no more. I was paralysed with fear, and lay under the clothes for a long time in an agony of terror, and nearly suffocated with heat.

'Fifteen years later, I met my cousin, the son of the house, who had been abroad, and was now staying with my father. I happened to mention to him the nightmare I had had in his father's house in Tyrone, and described the room in which it had happened. To my astonishment, he declared that he had had a similar experience in the same room. Furthermore, every time he slept in that room the same thing happened. The only difference between his experience and mine was that the black dog appeared to him with an old woman. He said he was not asleep when he saw them.

'About a week later his sister came to see me. Without saying anything about the black dog, I began to talk to her about her old home, and it soon transpired that she had had a similar experience in that room, except that, as in my experience, only the dog had appeared to her.'

The 'Dobhar Chu' of Lough Mask

'Chu' is Irish for dog, but in his *Description of West Connaught* (1684), Roderick O'Flaherty refers to the beast seen in Lough Mask not as a 'water dog' but as an 'Irish crocodile'. He described the experience of a man who was walking by the side of the lough when he saw far off in the water what appeared to be the head of a swimming creature. He assumed it to be an otter. The head then disappeared as the creature dived, and he thought no more of it. But, swimming under the water, the creature made straight for the man, came scrambling out on to the shore and tried to seize him and drag him into the lough. It was only with great difficulty that he pulled himself away and made his escape.

The Bear

One of Lady Gregory's contributors told this story:

'One time I was at the fair in Ballinasloe, and I but a young lad at the time, and a comrade with me that was but a young lad too. We brought in the sheep the Monday evening, and they were sold the Tuesday morning, and the master bid us to go home on the train.

'"Are we to get no good at all out of the fair?" said my comrade. "Let us stop," says he, "and get the good of it and

go back by the mail train." So we went through the fair
together and went to a dance, and the master never
knew, and we went home on the mail train together.

We got out at Woodlawn and we were going home,
and we heard a sort of a groaning and we could see
nothing, and the boy that was with me was frightened, for though he was a strong boy, he was a timor-
ous man. We found then the groaning coming from
beyond the wall, and I went and put my two fists on
the wall and looked over it. There were two trees on
the other side of the wall, and I saw walking off and
down from one tree to the other, something that was
like a soldier or a sentry. The body was a man's body,
and there was a black suit on it, but it had the head of a
bear, the very head and *puss* of a bear. I asked what
was on him. "Don't speak to me, don't speak to me,"
he said, and he stopped by the tree and was groaning
and went away.'

The Seal Man

Off the Connemara coast, a fisherman killed a seal
one day, as it swam by his boat, thinking there was
one less to eat the fish he wanted to catch. When he
came in to the shore, it was night coming on, and as
he was desperate to have a smoke – 'dead with the
want of a blast of pipe' was how it was put – he went
to a house by the beach to ask for a burning coal from
the fire with which to light his pipe. A woman took
him in, and when he was well inside the room, he
saw a man stretched out on the bed, and the woman
said the man, 'Look till you see who this man is who

has come.' And the man lying on the bed looked up, and said, 'I know you, for I have the mark of your hand on me. And let you get out of this now,' he continued, 'as fast as you can, and it will be best with you.' And the woman, who appeared to be his daughter, said, 'I wonder how you would let him go as easy as that.' The fisherman made off without any delay, as fast as he could go. The man on the bed was the seal he had killed; but he was not dead, for he was of the Sheogues who could not be slain by a mortal.

'Pronc'

The family who took over a large, rambling house on the south side of Dublin had no notion that there was anything strange about it. It felt a friendly, comfortable, sunny sort of place. The period was the late nineteenth century. The two little girls of the family had a big bedroom at the rear of the house, as the younger child was an invalid and liked to have her sister share the room. But about a week after they had moved in, and when everyone was in bed, the elder girl came running up to her parents' bedroom, in great distress, crying that there was something rushing about in the girls' bedroom, which they couldn't see. The mother ran down, and even as she approached the open door, she heard the thuds of something apparently bounding about inside the room. But just before she went in, the noise stopped.

She spent the night with her two girls, and eventually they went to sleep. She remained awake and heard arise in one corner of the room what she described as 'a soft, sighing, whispering sound, which seemed to come out of the wall, and gradually crept all round the room till it reached where our beds were. Nearer it came, till it touched the bed, as if a winged beetle were fluttering against the quilt. All at once something heavy seemed to fall, and immediately the footfalls I had heard before sounded with a peculiar hollow thud, as if some animal (cat or dog) were jumping up and down; it lasted about ten minutes, and suddenly died away at the door. Next morning, both girls exactly described the first part of the noise as I had heard it, and it always came in the same way – an indescribable whisper in the beginning, and the conclusion a heavy thud.' The children named the invisible thing 'Pronc'.

Next day, the family were visited by an acquaintance who was a pet aversion of all of them; especially the younger child, who always became feverish and unwell when this individual was in the house. The mother observed that before this unwelcome and unwanted visitor came, there was always a manifestation from Pronc – as if the unseen thing was sensitive to other malevolent beings – and she always made a point of remaining at home on the day following any nocturnal noises.

One evening, she was sitting with her younger daughter by the fire, telling her a story, when the child gripped her hand and motioned towards the fire. There on the rug, its back to them, was a large cat, staring into the flickering firelight. Thinking it was her daughter's pet cat, the mother called out to it, 'Well, Peter-puss! Are you come in for your supper?' Later, she related, 'The creature turned, and looked full at us for a moment with eyes that were human, and a face, which though black, was still the face of an ugly woman! The mouth snarled at us for an instant, and a sad, angry howl came from it. And as we stared in horror, the thing vanished. We never saw it again.' Nevertheless, they left the house as soon as they could. Later, they discovered that fifty years before a woman had been robbed and murdered in the house, by her own son, and her body had been buried by him under the hearth-stone. Twenty years afterwards, her skeleton had been uncovered by tenants living in the house. They too had been troubled by the ghost, and though they gave the remains a proper burial, it seems that its presence could not be dislodged so easily.

The Night Horses

One of the Reverend John Seymour's correspondents wrote to him with an account of occurrences in a country house whose location, beyond its being in the North of Ireland, she did not divulge:

'I was awakened on several nights by hearing the tramp, tramp of horses' hooves. Sometimes it sounded as though they were walking on paving-stones, while at other times I had the impression that they were going round a large space, and as if someone was using a whip on them. I heard neighing, and champing of bits, and so formed the impression that they were carriage-horses. I did not mind it much at first, as I thought the stables must be near that part of the house.

'After hearing these noises several times, I began to get curious, so one morning I made a tour of the place. I found that the side of the house I occupied overlooked a neglected garden, which was mostly used for drying clothes. I also discovered that the stables were right at the back of the house, and so it would be impossible for me to hear any noises in that quarter; at any rate there was only one farm horse left, and this was securely fastened up every night. Also, there were no cobblestones round the yard. I mentioned what I had heard to the people of the house, but, as they would give me no satisfactory reply, I passed it over. I did not hear these noises every night.

'One night, I was startled out of my sleep by hearing a dreadful disturbance in the kitchen. It sounded as if the dish-covers were being taken off the wall and dashed violently on the flagged floor. At length I got up and opened the door of my bedroom, and just as I did so an appalling crash resounded through the house. I waited to see if there was any light to be seen, or footstep to be heard, but nobody was stirring. There was only one servant in the house, the other persons being my host, his wife, and a baby, who had all retired early.

'Next morning, I described the noises in the kitchen to the servant, and she said she had often heard them. I then told her about the tramping of horses. She replied that she herself had never heard it, but that other persons who had occupied my room had had experiences similar to mine. I asked her was there any explanation, to which she replied there was not, except that a story was told of a gentleman who had lived there some years ago, who was very much addicted to racing and gambling, and that he was shot one night in that house. For the remainder of my visit, I was removed to another part of the house, and I heard no more noises.'

The Killackee Cat

The old dower house at Killackee was bought in 1968 by the artist Margaret O'Brien and her husband Nicholas. There was much that needed doing to the house, and they had a team of workmen engaged on renovation and redecoration. When the workmen began to complain of a strange presence in the house – a big, black cat – she dismissed the story. But one day she saw it herself, inside the house when all doors to the outside were locked – a huge, jet-black cat, about as big as a medium-sized dog. The beast vanished, but soon afterwards one of the workmen, Thomas McAssey, at work in a room by himself, felt the air suddenly grow cold. He looked around but saw nothing. From beyond the open door, however, came a sound of low and threatening growls. Then a dark figure appeared in the doorway. He spoke to it, but a growl was the only answer. Mrs O'Brien had the house exorcized, which appeared to get rid of the cat-spirit, though other manifestations were said to trouble the place still.

The Rat of Howth Castle

The rat, sometimes said to be a white rat, was reputed to appear when evil threatened the House of St Laurence. Its first appearance was in the seventeenth century, to a Lord of Howth.

On a stormy winter evening, a ship was seen in difficulties in Howth Bay. Thrown on the rocks by an easterly gale, she broke up while the watchers on shore could do nothing to reach her. Every soul on board was presumed to have drowned, but, in the morning, a woman was found clinging to some wreckage that had been washed up on to the beach. More dead than alive, she was brought to Howth Castle, and cared for.

When the Earl of Howth came to see her, he was struck by her pallor and her beauty. Once she had recovered from the ordeal, he pressed her to stay on in the castle, and she did. Soon he was madly in love with her, but although he pressed her often to marry him, she always refused, and begged him to look for some other bride.

At last, driven by vexation and frustration, he did so, and found a bride from a nearby family. The lady from the sea gave him a ribbon, its material interwoven with strange words and signs, and asked him to wear it always on his wrist, in memory of her. Soon afterwards she left Howth Castle, and nobody knew where she had gone.

The Earl's new bride was intrigued by the ribbon, which he wore night and day. One night, soon after they were married, she undid it from his wrist as he lay sleeping in their chamber, and took it over to the fire, to look at it more closely. By ill luck she dropped it; it was sucked into the flames and immediately burned. When Lord Howth discovered its loss, he was very distressed.

'Ill fortune will come of this,' he said.

Not long after that, while a feast was going on in the castle hall, the dogs of the place chased a rat into the room. The hunted beast sprang up on the table, right in front of the Lord of Howth. Its posture and expression seemed so pleading that he saved it from the dogs. From then on, much to the distaste of his wife and family, the rat became his pet. Wherever he went, even if he did not bring it, it seemed to follow him. Even to France, where he went with his brother on a tour. The rat had been left behind, but as they sat by the fire in a Marseilles hotel, it appeared, soaked and limping, as if it had travelled a great way. Exasperated, his brother took a heavy poker and, before he could be stopped, killed the animal.

'You have murdered me!' cried the Earl.

That same night, he died. But the rat still haunts the castle.

The Beasts of Tuamgraney

By Tuamgraney in County Clare is a wooded hollow that is said to be haunted, especially around the end of October, when Hallowe'en is near. At that time, the residents used to avoid the area, but one young man, either sceptical or forgetful, went walking there in late October. It was a peaceful autumn day. Carrying a stout stick, he walked downhill among the trees. There did not seem to be anything threatening in the quiet woodland but despite this, a sense of acute foreboding came upon him quite suddenly – a combination of fear and a strange, deep sadness. He paused for a moment, and almost decided to turn back, then dismissed the feeling as imagination and pressed onwards. But he went more cautiously now and was unable to rid himself of the sense of being on forbidden and dangerous ground. The trees seemed more numerous and more densely packed than he remembered.

Walking softly along the indistinct and overgrown path, he saw ahead of him that the wood was bathed in a dim, unnatural light. Thoughts and memories came to him, of how groves like this were used in past times for pagan rites and ceremonies. Perhaps blood sacrifices had been offered up here, in this place that was now so still, so ominously breathless and silent. As he made his way slowly along, there was a movement in the bushes ahead and he saw a dog among the leaves – a black dog, its size hard to gauge in the shadows, but with an expression of malevolence in its red eyes. Some stray, he said to himself, but his heart was beating wildly. The creature's abrupt disappearance did nothing to allay his fears. Then he jumped with fright as something sprang into his path. It was a hare, a big, black hare, and red-eyed like the dog. For a moment it looked at him, and again he felt a current of malice flow towards him. The hare bounded away into the undergrowth, and now a cat appeared, the colour of straw. It faced him on the path, its back arched, fangs bared, eyes glaring, before it too retreated into the shadows. He would have turned and fled, but now the ground beneath his feet was rising upwards, and he felt it was quicker to press on than to go back. But his experiences were not yet over.

The way led into a clearing. Oncoming evening made the sky here almost as dark as the forest cover had been, but he saw that the clearing was occupied. Two animals were struggling there, one a deer hind, the other a black ram with ferocious eyes and massive curled horns. The deer sank to its side, wounded and exhausted, and the young man caught what seemed to be a look of appeal in its eyes. Brandishing his stick, he ran forward and attempted to beat off the ram. But as he struck, he found his blow connected with nothing but empty air. Yet when the ram turned on him, he felt a savage buffet as the massive horned head butted him. He fell to the ground, winded, and blacked out for a moment. When he came to, the scene was deserted; also, to his surprise, there were only a few trees instead of dense woodland surrounding the clearing. But as he got to his feet, his sides were still aching from the ram's horns, and he made his way slowly home.

At home, he told his story as if it had been a dream, but an uncle of his confirmed that others too had stumbled into the phantom forest around that time of year.

APPARITIONS

The Red Shirts

Apparitions are as old as Irish legend. Often they are death-warnings. In one of the Cuchulain stories, *Cuchulain of Muirthemne*, it is told how Cuchulain was travelling with Cathbad the Druid, and they came to a ford where they saw a young girl, yellow-haired, thin and white-skinned, washing and washing in the stream at clothing that was stained a bloody red, and, all the time as she beat the washing, she was crying out and keening.

'Little hound,' said Cathbad, 'do you see what it is that young girl is doing? It is your red clothes she is washing, and crying as she washes them, because she knows you are going to your death against Maeve's great army.'

The Recently Dead

In his book, *Passing the Time*, studying the life of a Fermanagh community, Henry Glassie recounts the experience of a group of men in or about 1949. One of them, a man from Inishmore, County Fermanagh, had been driving home at night and had an accident on the viaduct over Upper Lough Erne. Some others helped him, and he then gave them a lift in his car. As they were driving along a country lane, a man recently dead, known to them all, stepped out into the glare of the headlights. No matter which way the driver tried to swerve, the figure stayed in front, until they came to a crossroads, where the driver twisted the wheel sharply, and they escaped. The story was re-counted by one Hugh Nolan, and was backed up by the brother of one of the men who had been in the car.

The Eavesdropping Charwoman

One of the Reverend John Seymour's collection of ghostly reminiscences was from a Dublin lady, Mrs Kelly, who lived in one of the grand squares of the city. Her house was haunted by what appeared to be the figure of a domestic servant or charwoman, 'a tall, stout, elderly woman wearing a bonnet and old-fashioned mantle. She had grey hair, and a benign and amiable expression.'

Despite the expresssion, a sense of growing fear came over Mrs Kelly, and she found herself backing against the wall, until the vision eventually faded. The same terror was aroused when the apparition reap-peared sporadically, in different parts of the house, over a period of ten years. On the last occasion, Mr Kelly had been singing in a concert, and he and his wife sat eating a late supper, and discussing the con-cert. When she left the room, Mrs Kelly discovered her old lady 'standing on the mat outside with her head bent towards the door in the attitude of listening. I called out loudly and my husband rushed to my side. That was the last time I have seen her.'

This ghost had the behaviour of an old retainer of settled habits, who did not like change or strangers.

When visitors came to stay, the chairs in the guest room were often found turned over. She also shared the propensity of ghosts to make knocking sounds, to such an extent that the owner of the house next door asked Mr Kelly why he chose such unsociable hours to put up pictures.

The Kilkenny Invalid

The semblance of a woman on crutches has been seen on numerous occasions in the city of Kilkenny. Described as tall and thin, wearing a long coat, and with long, white hair, she appeared in the vicinity of St John's Parochial Hall. A nurse and her boyfried saw the figure in May 1967; it came past their parked car, then disappeared. When the startled couple drove on for a few yards and stopped again, the same thing happened.

The Bog of Allen Shapes

Not all apparitions are instantly recognisable. In the dreary, featureless flats of the Bog of Allen, especially in the days before much of it was drained and reclaimed for cultivation, there were strange manifestations. Vague, indistinct shapes could sometimes be seen by travellers, only a little darker than the grey sky itself, lingering among the peaty pools and black sumps of the surface. From a distance they looked like human figures, and so got a bad name for luring unsuspecting wayfarers into the treacherous depths of the bog. Here, there were areas of soft mud, of unknown depth, where they would be swallowed up and die a hideous choking death as the slime engulfed them. But it may be that there was no such intention in this.

One traveller recorded an experience that might confirm this impression. Walking in the Bog of Allen, on a well-known path, he was overtaken by a heavy rainstorm. The sky was so darkened by clouds that he feared he would lose the path. Then in the distance he saw a low cabin, an indistinct shape in the rain. Hoping for shelter from the downpour, he made his way towards it. As he came near, he saw it was a derelict house, long-abandoned, the door an empty hole, with no glass in any of its windows, and the roof half-collapsed. Nevertheless, it offered some respite, and he went in.

Standing in the doorway, eating his rain-soaked sandwiches, he looked out, hoping to see the sky brighten. Not far away, the dark loops of a stream wound their way across the bog-land. At one point on the stream-bank, he saw what appeared to be a dark patch of haze, like fog, and yet not fog. Knowing that the bog-land had strange atmospherics of its own, he was not unduly puzzled, and yet it gave him a somewhat eerie feeling. This feeling was greatly intensified when he saw that the hazy patch was moving over the surface of the bog in his direction. There was a sense of purpose in that steady movement that made him feel something was directing its course straight at him; something that was not friendly to humanity. As happens in a nightmare, he felt himself unable to move from the doorway as the darkness loomed up, blotting out everything else in the landscape.

As it reached him, his terror reached a climax. It was completely dark, and he seemed to feel arms brushing past him. He was convinced that something terrible was about to happen to him. But then, suddenly, it was gone. It had moved on, through the ruined house and onward into the expanse of bogland beyond. Gulping and gasping for breath, he staggered to the corner of the house, oblivious of the still pouring rain, to see it dwindle and vanish into the distance. Whatever it was, some cold, lonely, shapeless spirit of the marsh, it had no more concern for him than if it had been the wind. But the terror that it induced was very far from natural.

The Boy from the Sea

In a typical outing for a well-to-do household in Edwardian Belfast, the Smyth family set off early one day in July 1910 on a train and tramway excursion to the Giant's Causeway. The party consisted of Mr Smyth, a linen-works manager, his wife, two teenage daughters, his son Charles, aged nine, and their maid, Kate Kennedy. They reached the Causeway shortly before lunch on a fine, sunny day. It was a city holiday, and there were numerous other groups. The Smyths walked some way along, below the cliffs, to a quieter area, and settled down on their rugs to enjoy a picnic lunch from the baskets they had brought with them. After the lunch, Mr and Mrs Smyth decided to take a little nap, leaving Kate to supervise the children. Charles, an adventurous boy, was especially warned to be careful, in jumping about on the many levels of the rock formations. The girls did not go far away, and Kate kept a lookout for the boy, but among the pillars of varying height, it was very hard to keep him in view. The last time she saw him, he seemed to be making his way down to the water's edge, and she called to him to take care; he waved back jauntily.

Suddenly, Mrs Smyth sat up.

'Charles!' she said, 'Something's happened!'

'No, he's fine,' said Kate. 'I saw him just a moment ago.'

But when they both stood up and looked around, they could not see the boy. Alarmed, they woke Mr Smyth, who hurried down towards the sea. Although it was a calm day, there was a smooth swell on the sea, which rose and fell almost silently among the rocks, with hardly any breaking or spray. It was a deep, dark blue, almost ultramarine in colour. There was something sinister in the heavy, noiseless movement which struck a deep chord of unease in him. Distraught by now, the whole family combed the area, and Kate rushed up to the tramway terminal to get further help. But the boy had disappeared. A few days later, his body was found about three miles along the coast. It was assumed he had lost his footing and slipped into a deep channel, and been carried away by the current of the outgoing tide.

Soon after that sad event, reports began to be heard, of people who had seen a small boy in a sailor suit, down by the water's edge. One young couple almost stumbled on him as they negotiated the rock pillars. They thought that he seemed to be looking for someone. 'Are you lost?' the man asked. Then they noticed that his face was deadly pale, and his clothes seemed to be soaking wet. And then – he vanished. Since then, the boy from the sea has been seen on a few rare occasions.

The Women of Springhill

Springhill, in County Londonderry, is a handsome seventeenth-century house, long inhabited by a family who came originally from Ayrshire in Scotland. How long it has been haunted, no one knows. Late in the nineteenth century, a Miss Wilson saw a tall female figure standing at the top of the main staircase. The figure approached a door on the landing, threw up its hands in an expressive gesture of grief, then disappeared from the watcher's sight. Not long after that another lady, Miss Hamilton, visiting the house, saw a group of servants gathered in front of a door, talking and pointing towards it. The door suddenly opened, apparently of its own volition, and light streamed out. On a later visit, Miss Hamilton observed that this door had been papered over by the owners of the house. It was also recorded that a governess, hired to teach the children of the house, overheard her charges talking in the next room. When she went to see who they were talking to, there was no one, but from their description she realized they had been talking to a lady ghost. Another observer, a man this time, saw a spectral woman in black standing at the foot of the stairs. The man, Terry Duffy, in charge of running the estate, made some investigations and concluded that he had seen the widow of Colonel Conyngham, a soldier of the Crimean War period (1852). The portrait of the same lady hung in the house. Later it disappeared, then was mysteriously sent back wrapped in brown paper, before it finally disappeared for good.

Like so many strange manifestations in Irish houses, there is clearly some mystery – or mysteries – at the bottom of these happenings at Springhill, which have never been fully explored.

The Third Policeman

In the 1880s, during a fine, moonlit night, two constables of the Royal Irish Constabulary were sent to walk with despatches to the next police station, some five miles distant. The air was still and clear, with a touch of frost. It did not take them long to reach their destination, and as they approached it, they saw another policeman appear on the road ahead of them. The police station was on one side of the road, and a whitethorn hedge at the other.

It was as if this third officer had stepped out from the hedge. He looked towards the two others, then stepped towards the station and disappeared into its shadow. The aproaching policemen assumed he was on guard duty inside, and had simply come out for a breath of air. Both of them saw him clearly – a stoutly built, bareheaded man, with a pale, round face and mutton-chop whiskers, and his tunic open at the front.

However, when the two constables got to the station door, they found it was locked and bolted against them. It took prolonged knocking to rouse someone inside. When they were finally admitted, there was no sign of the whiskered constable, nor could he have got in and locked the door in the time they took to approach. They soon found that no one had been posted on guard, and realized that whoever or whatever they had seen, it was not a flesh-and-blood colleague. Fearing ridicule, they said nothing. It was only some years later that they learned that a policeman had been found dead in the snow, not far from the station.

The White Light of Crom

In Crom Bay, in Upper Lough Erne, a strange white light is sometimes seen. One eye-witness described it as 'a round ball of light, about twice the size of a football. It was dusk, and it lit up brilliantly the trees between the lake and the castle (Crom Castle, home of the Crichton family) as it raced past over the surface of the water.' On another occasion in the evening, two or three of the castle gardeners were rowing across the lake from the castle to their homes when the light appeared, moving swiftly in their direction. They promptly reversed oars, pulled hard back to the shore, and ran for their lives.

Mr Hyslop, at one time the head gardener at Crom, related his experience:

'The night was dark and the lake very rough and I

had gone down to the quay with the district nurse to see her into the boat. Knowing her to be a coward on the water, I was unhappy at the nurse crossing over to her home, so my attention was all on her. When we reached the quay, I noticed a light in the middle of the lake, slightly left of the old castle. This rather surprised me, as I thought the water too rough for fishermen. I looked at it for a second or two, and noticed that there was no reflection on the water, or rays from the light. Although the lake was rough, the light appeared to be quite steady, and only a foot or so above the water. It was a beautiful golden colour and about the size of a motor headlamp. It may have been visible before I went down to the quay, but it disappeared soon afterwards, and while my attention was on the boat.'

The Bloody Bridge

The years from 1641 onwards were a period of great troubles and disturbance in the north of Ireland. The impending war between the supporters of King Charles I and those of the London Parliament was already a cause of strife and bloodshed. Added to this was the still-continuing struggle between the Irish inhabitants of the region and the 'planted' English and Scottish settlers who for a generation had been established in the province of Ulster. Atrocities were committed by both sides.

One of the most notorius of these was the massacre that happened at the 'Bloody Bridge' in 1641. A large number of women and children of the 'planters' had been rounded up and were being led away from their farms and homesteads. As they went, it was claimed that they were set upon, and robbed of any valuables they carried, even of their clothing. It was mid-November, and bitterly cold. As the crowd, whose numbers have been estimated at anything between eighty and three hundred and eighty, moved on to the narrow wooden bridge over the River Bann at Portadown, they were stopped. Standing on the planks, with the swift-flowing river beneath them, they saw that their captors were heaping up brush-wood and kindling at each end of the bridge. It was impossible to get off, except by a suicidal plunge into the river. Soon the old bridge was burning furiously. All the women and children perished, in the flames and smoke, or in the water.

In Dublin in 1642, witnesses of the massacre testi-fied to what they had seen. Many macabre incidents were noted after the event. According to some accounts, the river ran red, as if with blood, for weeks. Heads were seen in the water, bobbing about, impos-sible to capture with a net or grapple. In the space once spanned by the bridge, the figure of a woman and baby was seen, said to be urging the government troops on to avenge the deaths that had happened there.

The vengeance taken was as gruesome and pitiless as the massacre itself. Though some have doubted its extent, or even its existence, there seems no doubt that a dark deed was done at the 'Bloody Bridge' in 1641.

Jack Hayson

The Hayson family lived in Waterford, in the late nineteenth century. Their house was on the quay, just by the River Suir and the harbour. It was on Christmas Eve that Eli Hayson saw and heard the ghost of his twin brother, Jack. Jack was a seaman, and his ship, the *Thomas Emery*, was moored at Cork, fifty miles away. But when Eli, just about to go to bed, heard the sound of running feet outside, and looked out of the window on to the moonlit quay, he saw Jack come running towards the house from the direction of the harbour. Eli was on the point of leaving his window to open the front door for his brother, when he saw three other figures following Jack in pursuit. He tried to shout, but could not make himself heard. Nor could he move, as he saw Jack, in his seaman's jersey and trousers, come right up to the house. But then the pursuing figures closed in on him. In the bright moonlight, Eli saw his brother's upturned face, and heard him cry, 'For God's sake, help me!' Still he could not move. Only when a cloud moved across the face of the moon and everything went dark, was the spell lifted. He hurried down and opened the door, but the quay was deserted.

Baffled, and believing he had had some kind of waking nightmare, Eli went to bed. But next day the Haysons received the message that Jack was drowned, having sleepwalked off the side of his ship. At the inquest in Cork, the twins' father confirmed that neither of his sons had ever been sleepwalkers. But several of the crew testified that they had seen Jack, on numerous occasions, get up from his bunk, dress, and walk about the ship's deck, still fast asleep. The verdict was of accidental death by drowning. But, in the light of his strange vision, Eli and his family were by no means satisfied that the true cause of Jack's death had been established. As the years went by, it remained a mystery.

It was twenty years later that Eli discovered the truth about his brother's fate. He had occasion to make business trips to Cork, and usually had a drink in the same bar each time. On one occasion, the barman gave him a message. An old man in the town wanted to see him, with some personal information. Going to the address given, Eli was received by an ancient man, Mr Webster, who welcomed him in. After some desultory talk, old Webster told his story. His own son, Tom, had been a nightwatchman at the warehouses on the quay at Cork. Tom had died shortly before, but had told his father something that had been on his conscience for a long time.

One Christmas Eve, he had been sitting half-dozing at his brazier, when he heard the sound of stealthy footsteps. Looking up, he was startled and frightened to see three grotesque figures pass along, close to the edge of the quay. Their bodies were those of men, dressed like sailors, but two of them had the heads of apes, and one that of a deer. Tom crept to the corner of a nearby shed and gazed after them in fear and wonderment. He saw the three figures going down some steps to the water, then pulling away in a dinghy, bound for one of the ships moored in the river.

The moon was bright, and the ship was near. Venturing close to the water's edge, he was gazing intently over the moonlit water, when he was chilled by a scream of terror. A man appeared on the deck, and ran wildly along it, followed in a trice by the three bizarre figures. As they closed in on their quarry, the watcher heard him cry out, 'For God's sake, help me!' A moment later there was a splash. The young man had jumped overboard. Tom could hear him for a moment or two, flailing helplessly in the water, but he himself was frozen to the spot by terror. And then, there was only silence. But Tom was horror-struck to see the three pursuers raise their hands to their heads and, as it seemed, tear off their own faces, before they looked over the side. Then he realized they had been wearing masks.

'He went to the inquest,' said old Webster. 'But he was terrified that if he said anything, they would come for him too. So he said nothing. But it was always on his conscience that he had seen Jack Hayson die, and done nothing to stop it.'

Eli returned home, full of thoughts of that night, twenty years before, when he had seen his brother come running, in vain, to his home. What the motives of the assailants were – revenge maybe, or even only a vicious practical joke – he never discovered.

'Covered All Over with Yellow Spots'

The ghost-hunter Elliott O'Donnell saw a bizarre apparition at the age of five. His nurse had put him to bed, and she had just gone, when the door slowly opened and there entered a creature of extraordinary appearance. O'Donnell recorded the experience and his own reaction:

'It was about five feet and ten inches in height, nude, and covered all over with yellow spots. It had a big, out-of-proportion head and bright eyes which regarded me with an expression which utterly baffles description: it was so entirely enigmatical and perplexing. Yet I was not at all frightened; I was merely puzzled for the thing did not appear to be hostile but merely ominous. Young though I was, I felt it was there for a purpose and that it had something to do with my fate and future and I have thought so ever since. It remained stationary, gazing at me for some seconds, and then left the room in the same, noiseless, stealthy manner in which it had entered. I never saw it or anything like it again.'

Later, in the same house, O'Donnell observed other phenomena. Looking out from an upstairs window, he saw two figures approaching, to all appearances two perfectly normal people. They came up the path and disappeared from view, heading for the back door. Then knocking was heard on the back door. The boy went to look out at the back, but saw no one at the back doorstep, though the knocking on the door could still be heard. When he asked the servants why they had not answered the door, they said. 'What is the good? There will be no one there. We know that knocking.'

Samuel Penrose
Church of Ireland clergymen appear to have had more

of a sense of impersonal occult forces – neither good nor evil – than their Catholic parish priest counter-parts. One, who corresponded with the Reverend John Seymour, wrote of the apparition he saw of one of his parishioners, Samuel Penrose, just after Penrose's death. Penrose was a returned emigrant from Argentina, a builder's carpenter, and a very respectable man of sincere religious feelings.

'Soon after his return, he met with one or two rather severe accidents, and had a strong impression that a fatal one would happen to him before long; and so it came to pass. A scaffolding gave way one day, and precipitated him on to a flagged stone floor. Although he did not die immediately, his injuries proved fatal and he died in a Cork hospital soon after his admission. I went to Cork to offficiate at his funeral. About noon the next day, I was standing at my hall door, and the form of poor Sam, the upper half of it, seemed to pass before me. He looked peaceful and happy – it was a momentary vision, but perfectly distinct.'

The writer goes on to comment that the 'half-only' appearance of the figure, which had seemed odd, was quite usual in such experiences according to the authoritative writer, F. W. H. Myers, who had analysed many similar ones.

Ghost in a Tree

An old gardener told Elliott O'Donnell about a tree ghost he had seen as a boy. He had been walking across a field with his father and another man, when all three of them saw something appear from beneath the branches of an old elm tree. The figure was in-substantial. However, despite its haziness, they could make out the likeness of a man, though the arms were unusually long and there was something odd, not quite right, about the head and the feet. The figure was tall and thin, and naked. The two men and the boy hurried away without looking more. The old man told O'Donnell that he believed elms and birches to be the trees most liable to house spirit presences.

A Galway Ghost

In 1965, the actor-manager Mícheál MacLiammoir was performing in the city of Galway. With the theatre manager, he was invited to lunch one day by the proprietor of a local porcelain factory and his wife. As they left the house to walk to the nearby factory, MacLiammoir, who was sensitive to the paranormal, suddenly said, 'There is a woman walking through this place who is not of this earth, and with her is a dog.'

The manager gave him a very strange look, but mentioned MacLiammoir's remark to the factory-owner. 'Yes,' said the latter, 'it's true that the place is supposed to be haunted by a woman who was murdered here, many years ago, and there was a dog which tried to protect her.

Le Baiser

The Galway ghost was by no means MacLiammoir's only encounter with the supernatural. In October 1934, he was returning from America on an Atlantic liner. Early one morning, as he was walking round the empty deck, he heard someone singing. First he recognized the song, an old French one, *Le Baiser* ('the kiss') and then he recognized the voice of the singer. It was his sister. Gradually it seemed to him as though she were walking round the deck with him. He recalled:

'We walked around and around, and I began singing the song myself. I was extraordinarily happy, for I hadn't seen her for many years. She was a sister I loved very much.'

Five days later, when he got back to Ireland, he was met by his aunt, who said she had sad news to give him. His sister had died, just five days before.

Dan's Last Jar

The countryside west of Cookstown, County Tyrone, was a prime area for the manufacture of illicit whiskey well into the 1930s, if not later. 'Wee still' is the local name for *poitín*, and there are many local stories about its makers and their escapades. But only one still, or its site, is haunted. Out on the peat moss, or in secret places on the hillsides, is where they were set up in those days. One well-known maker (his name is given as Dan McIlhenny or McIlvicken) had an exceptionally good location, in a deep, dry hollow in the moss. He had covered this with branches and cut twigs of heather, so that it looked just like a flat patch of dead, dry heather. But in the middle, he had set an iron grid, so that the smoke from his fire could escape. Like some other *poitín*-makers, he had had the clever idea of getting his lookout men to make a peat fire on top of this iron grating. If any busybody or RUC man came along, they would see a young fellow sitting harmlessly by a smoking fire, passing the time with his mates. Most of the time, of course, the fire was kept low, and part of the grid open, to let the smoke from the still come out. Unfortunately, one day, the lookouts neglected their task and left the grating completely covered up. The atmosphere below became gradually thicker and thicker, until Dan, intent on minding his brew, first became unconscious and then died of asphyxiation. The discovery of his body caused terrible consternation. It was brought home and cleaned up of soot, and a co-operative doctor found to ascribe the fatality to heart failure. Dan was duly 'waked' and buried.

But despite his fate, his distilling site was too good to abandon, especially with all its equipment, so, after a decent interval, some of his cronies began to use it again. But, inevitably, rumours of the true cause of Dan's death had spread around, and reached the ears of the RUC.

A discreet watch was kept on the place, and when the smoke was seen rising, a little troop of police rose out of the heather. Seeing them come, the lookouts immediately built peat up over their fireplace. But to their surprise, when the policemen were still about a hundred yards away, they hesitated, and stopped. For a moment they looked at one another, then they turned and ran. Soon they were out of sight over the hill. Greatly relieved, the *poitín*-makers cleared their incriminating evidence away on peat sledges as fast as they could.

It was only later that they learned what had caused the policemen to turn tail. While they themselves had seen nothing untowards, in front of the posse of police had appeared a terrifying figure, the form of Dan McIlhenny, his face a ghastly pale beneath streaks of soot, his eyes red and glaring. In the crook of one arm, he held an earthenware crock of familiar form; in the other he held a stout blackthorn stick. Seeing this apparition of a well-known man whom they knew to be dead and buried, the policemen were struck with fear. As he glided towards them, seeming to loom larger and larger, their terror got the better of them, and they bolted.

The news of this event was celebrated by the *poitín*-makers with a second and even finer wake for their dead companion, with many toasts to his memory. By the end of it, Dan's last jar was well and truly empty.

THE BANSHEE

Not for You

It was not everyone whose death was presaged by the banshee. Once upon a time in Dingle, there were a lot of the Hussey family living in John Street, most of them merchants in a small way. One night, in the very middle of the darkest time, the banshee was heard wailing outside. In every house, there were anxious faces and worried meetings. Someone was going to die – but who? But then, to their surprise, the banshee stopped her crying and they heard her voice outside, telling them in Irish:

> 'Listen, listen, you hoarding traders,
> You are not in danger,
> A banshee never keened your kind.'

The next day, they heard that a gentleman in the town, also of the name of Hussey, had died that night.

A Sceptic Converted . . .

In her scholarly book, *The Banshee*, from which the previous story comes, Patricia Lysaght also relates the story of a County Offaly man who 'did not believe in the banshee until it came home to me that there is such a thing as the banshee. I proved it. I was putting in the cows one evening. We had three cows and I put in a mash for one of the cows. When I was coming down with the cows, I heard a terrible cry, and didn't I run down. I thought someone was after meeting with an accident. But there was nothing wrong with any beast or human.

'Now, when we seen that nothing happened, it kind of left our heads what occurred. But that same evening, I heard the cry, Mary Anne [the narrator's sister] had a letter in her pocket. She took out the letter which was from a brother of ours who was in North America. Martin was his name. And Martin said in the letter that another brother of ours had gone to hospital, he wasn't so well. About three weeks after, we got word that he was dead. So it would appear that at the time we heard the terrible cry, our brother, Mike, was after dying. But I wouldn't believe such a thing unless it came home to me. And that's not such a terrible long time ago.'

. . . and Another

In Rylands, Newtowncunningham, there once lived a family named Dunn, and the wail of the banshee was heard before the death of any member of it.

A local clergyman thought this was all nonsense, until he was called to the bedside of a dying Miss Dunn. Her friends sat around. He joined the company, and led a prayer. After it, he was very surprised to hear, in the distance, a wail, as of someone in distress. The others heard it too. Shortly afterwards, Miss Dunn died. From that time onwards, the clergyman often told the story, remarking in a slight misquotation of Shakespeare's *Hamlet*, 'There are more things in heaven and earth than are dreamt of in your philosophy.'

Lament for the Harper

Although some sources claim that the banshee cries only for those born into old Irish families with the Mac or O' prefix, there are many accounts that challenge this. One tells of the Reverend Charles Bunworth, an eighteenth-century rector of Buttevant, County Cork. He had the unusual accomplishment – for a clergyman – of being able to play superbly on the Irish harp. Perhaps it was his sympathy for this traditional instrument that won him the attention of the banshee. The old man was ill, but not considered in a dangerous condition, when his herdsman, Kavanagh, who had been sent to Mallow to pick up some medicine, came back in a highly agitated state.

He told the rector's daughter, Miss Elizabeth Bunworth, that all the way back he had been accompanied by the keening of a banshee, who had mentioned the rector's name many times. He described her as 'keening, and screeching, and clapping her hands, by my side every step of the way, with her long white hair falling about her shoulders.' At Elizabeth's request, he said nothing about his experience.

But a few nights later, the old man, whose condition had got a little worse, was being watched over by an elderly female relation, when a sound was heard from outside, as of a woman moaning close to the window. Some of those in the house went out, to identify the source, but nothing was to be seen or heard. Yet, when they came back in, those inside the house assured them that the moaning had gone on, with clapping of hands, all the time they were out. And when they were back inside, they heard it again themselves. The condition of the sick man grew rapidly worse, and late that night, just before dawn, he died.

The One Who Did Not Hear

It was commonly said that the cry of the banshee was never heard by the person who was destined to die (there are some stories that dispute this). In one case, the girls of a family named O'Casey were out working in the bog, near a big hole called the Poll Rua ('red pool'), and the banshee began to cry from the edge of the bog. They all heard it quite clearly except for one of them. They wondered why she could not hear it when it was so clear to them. But on the way home, when they stopped at the Poll Rua to wash, this girl fell in, and was drowned.

The Song of the Banshee

In Spicer's *Strange Things Among Us* is the account of a banshee in the Kenealy family, which was heard mourning at the deathbed of a child, a young boy. His brother told the story of how the family and the doctor were gathered round the bed. It was a beautiful day, the window was open on a prospect of fields and hills, and sunlight streamed in. As they stood, they heard a strain of music, more entrancing than any normal human music. Accompanying it was the sound of a woman's voice, melancholy and yet melodious, and expressive of profound grief. For several moments they listened, and then the sound diminished and fell away. As it ceased to be audible, they saw that the sick boy was dying. The nurse who was there exclaimed, 'That is the banshee.' Everyone who was present agreed that nothing physical could have produced that singing.

The Banshee at Bunratty

Rathlaheen Cottage, a house near Bunratty Castle, was burned down in 1921 and later rebuilt. It had been haunted by unexplained knockings on doors and walls. In 1956, the banshee was heard here, immediately before a death occurred.

The Shane Castle Banshee

In Shane Castle, home of the O'Neills, there was at one time a room that was said to be the banshee's, and if her figure was seen to pace up and down inside it, crying and wringing her hands, then it was sure that some fatality in the family would follow. The banshee was described as a female figure of great beauty, tall, slender, dressed in green with a golden girdle, and with long golden hair and blue eyes.

The O'Donnell Banshee

In the course of several descriptions of the banshee,

Elliott O'Donnell recorded a personal experience. He and his wife were awakened about midnight by a series of agonising and heartrending cries. If they had any earthly resemblance, it seemed to him that they were like the cries of a woman in the greatest distress. At length, they died away in a long drawn-out sobbing wail.

Then, hearing whispering outside the bedroom door, O'Donnell got up and opened it, and found all the other occupants of the house gathered there, talking in hushed and frightened voices about the sound which they had all heard. At their request, O'Donnell searched through the house and went out into the grounds around, but he was not surprised to find nothing. He had recognized it as the cry of the banshee, and two or three days later heard that his aunt, also an O'Donnell, had died, on the day following the banshee's cry.

The O'Brien Banshee

In the seventeenth century, the Englishwoman, Anne, Lady Fanshawe, with her husband, was visiting Lady Honora O'Brien, daughter of the Earl of Thomond. She described in her memoirs, published in London in 1907, how she woke up one night, disturbed by the sound of a voice. She was in a four-poster bed, and, drawing aside its curtains, found she was looking straight at the window. There she saw a woman's face, pale and with huge sad eyes, looking in at her. Surrounding the face was a mass of red-gold hair, clearly visible in the moonlight. For some moments, the woman in the bed and the phantom at the window simply gazed at each other; then the apparition spoke.

Three times it 'spake loud, and in a tone I never heard, thrice, "Ahone", and then with a sigh, more like wind than breath, she vanished, and to me her body looked more like a thick cloud than substance.'

Lady Fanshawe woke her husband, who had slept through it all, and told him what she had seen. He did not mock her story, and told her that such apparitions were well known in Ireland. In the morning, Lady Honora informed her guests that a cousin of hers had died that night in the castle, at about two o'clock in the morning.

She herself had been up all night, but hoped that nothing had disturbed her visitors. Her reason for concern was that, whenever a member of the O'Brien family was at the point of death, the shape of a woman appeared, at the very room where she had inadvertently lodged her guests. According to Lady Honora, the banshee was the phantom of a woman who had been seduced and then murdered long ago by the castle's lord. The body had been buried in the ground beneath that window.

A Banshee in Italy

Elliott O'Donnell gives the story of a banshee that came to a family of Irish extraction living in Italy. They were the Neilsinis, descended from one of the O'Neills, an officer who had served in the French

King's Irish Brigade, and who had fled France after the revolution of 1789. In time, he became a wealthy count in Italy, and changed the family name to something more Italian-sounding. His great-grandson, who inherited the family's wealth and title, was cruising in his own yacht, with a party of friends, on one of the lakes in the Italian Alps. At one point, one of the guests asked him:

'Count, who is that strange-looking woman over there?'

Puzzled, the count replied that there were only the guests' own wives, and his stewardess on board.

'Oh, no,' said the other man, an army colonel. 'I have certainly seen someone else.' Then he gave a gasp, and put his hands before his eyes.

'Oh, my God, what a face!' he exclaimed.

'What is it?' asked the count, greatly concerned.

'It's gone,' replied the colonel. 'It was like nothing belonging to this world – a woman of no earthly type, with a queer-shaped, gleaming face, a mass of red hair, and eyes that would have been beautiful but for their expression, which was hellish. She wore a green hood, like an Irish peasant-woman.'

'That sounds like a banshee,' said one of the party.

'We are Irish,' said the count, and told them the story of his grandfather. 'It means the death of someone very closely associated with me. Pray God it is not my wife or my daughter.'

But it was he himself who was seized, two hours later, with an attack of angina pectoris, and he died later that same day.

Lord Rossmore's Banshee

A remarkable account of the banshee is given in Sir Jonah Barrington's *Personal Sketches of His Own Times*. Barrington, an Anglo-Irishman, was a lawyer and a member of the eighteenth-century Irish Parliament. The aged Lord Rossmore became a friend of his and invited Barrington and his wife as guests to his home, Mount Kennedy. Whilst they were there, their host was summoned away to Dublin Castle. Barrington's story goes as follows:

'Towards two in the morning, I was awakened by a sound of a very extraordinary nature. I listened: it occurred first at short intervals; it resembled neither a voice nor an instrument; it was softer than any voice and wilder than any music, and seemed to float in the air. I don't know wherefore, but my heart beat forcibly; the sound became still more plaintive, till it almost died in the air; when a sudden change, as if excited by a pang, changed its tone; it seemed descending. I felt every nerve tremble; it was not a natural sound, nor could I make out the point from whence it came.

'At length, I awakened Lady Barrington, who heard it as well as myself. She suggested it might be an Eolian harp, but to that instrument it bore no similitude; it was altogether a different character of sound. My wife at first appeared less affected than I, but subsequently she was more so.

'We now went to a large window in our bedrom, which looked directly upon a small garden underneath. The sound seemed then obviously to ascent from a grass plot immediately below our window. It continued; Lady Barrington requested I would call up her maid, which I did, and she was evidently more affected than either of us. The sounds lasted for more than half an hour. At last, a deep, heavy, throbbing sigh seemed to come from the spot, and was shortly succeeded by a sharp, lone cry, and by the distinct exclamation thrice repeated of "Rossmore, Rossmore, Rossmore!" '

The terrified maidservant fled from the window; Barrington and his wife were hardly less alarmed. With great difficulty, he persuaded Lady Barrington to return to bed. She asked him not to mention the experience to anyone, for she was sure they would be laughed at.

But at seven in the morning, there came a knock at their bedroom door. It was Lawler, Sir Jonah's servant. All he could say was, 'Oh, Lord, sir!'

'What is the matter?' asked Barrington, but Lawler only said, 'Oh, sir! Oh, sir!' Then Lord Rossmore's footman appeared. He announced to Sir Jonah that Lord Rossmore, having returned late in the night from Dublin Castle, had gone straight to bed, apparently in good health. Then at half past two, the valet who slept in the adjoining room, heard him make a strange noise, and hurried into the rom. He found Lord Rossmore dying, and before he could summon any aid, the peer was dead.

Sir Jonah Barrington's testimony is of special interest as, among the members of the 'ascendancy', the belief in banshees, ghosts and fairies was usually somewhat derided. Priding themselves on their robust common sense, they left such beliefs to the 'native Irish'.

(*See also* Banshee verse in the Appendix.)

CHANGELINGS

Mary Scannell's Baby

Mary Scannell was a young wife who lived with her husband not far from Castle Martyr, on the road from Cork to Youghal. She had a baby in the spring, and when it came to harvest time, she took the baby with her out to the fields, wrapped up in her brown cloak, and left her by the edge of the field. But when she came over to feed the child, she found a baby in the cloak that was not half the size of her own child, with a wizened little yellow face, that set up such a crying and screeching it was worse than a sick cat. Guessing what had happened, Mary picked up the little creature in the cloak, pretending to talk fondly to it, as if it were her own baby, and took herself as fast as she could to a wise woman.

The wise woman looked at the little yellow-faced thing, and told Mary Scannell not to feed it, and to pinch and slap it without mercy, no matter how loud it howled. This she did, and after a week of days and nights in which she got no rest and no sleep, with the screaming of the creature, at last a night came in which she fell asleep, and when she woke in the morning, her own baby was by her side again.

THE DEATH COACH

The Death Coach of Ballyduff

An anonymous correspondent from Clonmel passed this story to T. C. Croker, who included it in *Fairy Legends of Southern Ireland.*

'This was the experience of Michael Noonan, who lived near Ballyduff. One fine evening in summer, he was walking to Ballyduff to collect a pair of mended brogues from the shoemaker there. His way, on foot, took him by the river, past the derelict Hanlon's Mill. To his surprise, as he came by the mill, he heard the sound of hounds and huntsmen in full cry, yet there was nothing to be seen of them. Furthermore, he knew that the Duhallow hounds were out in quite another quarter of the countryside that day. His surprise turned to fear when he heard the "clack, clack" of the mill's mechanism at work, for the place had been abandoned for many a day. He positively ran the last of the distance to Ballyduff.

'When he got to the cobbler's shop, his fear subsided. There he found an old friend and near neighbour, Darby Haynes, a carrier by trade. Darby Haynes was waiting in town for his nephew to arrive, and he asked Michael if he would drive his cart home for him. Michael was pleased to agree, not fancying a return along the footpath that day, with the dark coming on.

'He drove home slowly under a clear sky, knowing

that the old horse had had a long day of it already. The moon rose, past a quarter towards the full, shedding brightness across the land. Lying back in the cart, Michael was idly watching the moon's reflection in a long pool that ran by the road's edge, when he saw it suddenly blanked off by a shadow. Wondering where the cloud had come from in that cloudless sky, he looked round, and saw a sight that chilled his blood.

'Drawing close alongside him, in utter silence, was a great black coach, drawn by six black horses. The coachman, high on his box, was draped in black. But the terrible thing was that neither he, nor his horses, had heads. The coach came abreast and passed rapidly by, the horses raising their hooves in a smart trot; the headless coachman laying the whip across their backs, and the wheels spinning round without a sound. The only noise came from his own horse and the squeaky axles of the cart that needed greasing. In a moment, the black coach had disappeared in the darkness of the next clump of trees. Michael Noonan, trembling, continued home, unharnessed the horse, put it out in the field, and put himself to his bed. Next morning, he was standing by the roadside, still perplexed and alarmed by the events of the previous day, when he saw Daniel Madden, huntsman to Mr Wrixon of Ballygibblin, come riding down the road at a mad pace. Stepping out, he waited for Dan to come up to him.

"For the love of God, don't stop me!" gasped the rider.

"Tell me what's the matter," said Michael. Madden gasped out the news that his master had taken a fit during the night and now lay close to death. He was riding to fetch the doctor. But maybe Michael could run across the fields and tell Kate Finnigan, the midwife, for she had medical skills that might help till the doctor got there. Michael went, as fast as he could go. But he already knew, and so it proved to be, that it was too late. The death coach had already claimed its latest passenger.'

The Death Coach of Derrymore

The death coach was also heard at Derrymore House, County Clare, in the late nineteenth century, when its owner, General Gore, lay dying. The doctor was awaited, and the general's wife, son and sister were at his bed. All clearly heard the sound of a coach drawing up outside. But then there was silence. No one got out. They hurried to the door of the house and looked out. There was nobody there; nothing to be seen. Receding down the avenue, however, they heard the crunch of wheels on gravel. Before the doctor arrived, the general was dead.

The Phantom Coach of the Vizes

The Vize family of County Cork were haunted by a coach drawn by headless horses and driven by a headless coachman. It was seen by Mrs Vize, in the late nineteenth century. With other members of the family, she was sitting in the drawing room of their house one evening, when they heard a vehicle approaching the house at a rapid pace. They sat up, expecting to find that some visitor had arrived. Gravel crunched as the carriage came up the drive; then the dogs in their kennels set up a howling and whining. Mrs Vize went to the window, to see who might be coming. As she looked out, she screamed, and fell fainting to the floor. When she was revived, she said she had seen a great black carriage, like a hearse, pulling up at the door. But the black horses drawing it had no heads, nor did the coachman who sat on the black-draped box. The other members of the family were too busy employed in caring for her to look out themselves, but they recalled hearing the sound of the carriage as it went away. A family death ensued a day or so after the visit of the phantom coach.

A Death Coach in County Limerick

This story was passed on through several generations of the Westropp family in County Limerick. In June 1806, Mr Ralph Westropp lay dying in his country house. The doctor had been called but had not yet arrived. As his three sons waited anxiously for the doctor to come, they heard a heavy rumbling sound outside, and hurried to the front door, in time to see a huge, dark coach draw up on the paved court at the front of the house. One of the sons went down the steps, expecting to see the doctor emerge, but the vehicle set off past him, and went racing down the avenue, which ran in a straight line to the gate which led out on to the road. Two of the young men ran after it, but they did not see it stop at the gate, yet when they came to the gate it was shut. The lodgekeeper had seen and heard nothing, and had certainly not let such a notable vehicle either in or out. Soon afterwards, the doctor arrived in his usual gig, but he could do nothing for the patient, who died a few hours later.

A number of other Irish families have experienced the phenomenon of the death coach. (*See also* a more humorous approach to this subject in the account of 'The Death Coach' in the Appendix, page 184.)

ECCLESIASTICAL GHOSTS

An Archbishop in Fancy Dress

One of the Anglican Archbishops of Dublin, the genial Richard Whately, was a man around whom stories seemed to accumulate. One strange story was of the Archbishop's ghost. Whately had owned a house in Dundrum, then on the outskirts of Dublin – a rambling old place. After his death, it was rented by a land agent and his wife.

One evening, as she was going down the wide staircase, the lady saw someone in front of her, whom she took to be one of her own sons, dressed up in fancy dress. The figure wore a wide-brimmed Spanish hat and a cloak.

She spoke to him, but he paid no attention, and went into the dining room. Annoyed by his lack of manners, she followed him in there, and was astonished to see a complete stranger facing her from the far side of the dining-table. His cloak was pulled up over the lower part of his face, and his hat-brim drawn down; but she could see his eyes looking out at her. He walked a little way round the table, and then vanished.

A friend of the lady once mentioned this experience to some nuns at the Loreto Convent. They in turn brought in an English nun, visiting from an English convent, who was most interested to hear the story. Later, she met the lady who had seen the ghost, and it then transpired that the English nun was one of Whately's relatives who had adopted the Catholic faith.

She told of a family legend that the old man used to appear in that house when any near relative of his died. Further research established that, on the day the lady had seen the hatted and cloaked figure, the Archbishop's daughter had died. The strange costume was explained by the fact that Whately had acquired the hat and cloak on a visit to Spain, and enjoyed garbing himself in them.

The Priest's Bedroom

A Church of Ireland minister in a country parish in County Galway woke up very early one morning, with the strong feeling that someone else was in his bedroom. Looking around, he saw an elderly man, with a red muffler about his neck, carrying a candle in one hand. Behind him was another figure, more indistinct, but definitely male. His three-year-old daughter was in her cot in the same room, and just as he began to feel he must still be dreaming, she called out, 'Oh, Papa – the man! The man!'

The minister came to the view that the apparition had been that of his predecessor in the parish, whom the description of the ghost resembled. He had been in the habit of wearing a red muffler. But the ghost made no attempt at communication, and did not reappear.

The Ghost in the Library

However, the most famous clerical ghost is Archbishop Marsh, who rejoiced in the unusual first name of Narcissus. He was the founder of the Dublin Library which bears his name, and his ghost is said to appear in it, apparently in search of a particular book. The Archbishop had a niece, who lived with him, and who was in love with the curate at Chapelizod. The Archbishop disapproved of the match, and the girl was obliged to carry on her courtship furtively. She and her lover used the Archbishop's library as a place to leave notes for each other, inserted in certain books. The final note was to make an assignation to meet for their elopement. This duly happened and the young couple were married in a tavern. Her uncle was greatly upset by the whole affair and never came to terms with his niece. He is said to revisit his library, looking always and in vain for illicit messages thrust between the covers of the many stately volumes in his collection.

The Ghost Room at Maynooth

In his book, *Window on Maynooth*, Father Denis Meehan mentions the existence of a haunted room at Maynooth College. One of the main blocks of the complex of buildings is Rhetoric House. 'For the curious, however, the most interesting feature of Rhetoric House will certainly be the ghost room. The two upper floors are altogether residential, and the ghost room is, or rather was, Room 2 on the top corridor. It is now an oratory of St Joseph. Legend, of course, is rife concerning the history of this room, but unfortunately everything happened so long ago that no one can now guarantee anything like accuracy. The incident, whatever it may have been, is at least dated to some extent by a Trustees' resolution of 23 October 1860: "That the President be authorized to convert Room 2 of the top corridor of Rhetoric House into an Oratory of St Joseph, and to fit up an Oratory of St Aloysius in the prayer hall of the Junior Students."

'The story, as it is commonly now detailed for the edification of susceptible freshmen, begins with a suicide. The student resident in this room killed himself one night. According to some he used a razor, but tellers of the story are not too careful about such details. The next inhabitant, it is alleged, felt irresistibly compelled to follow suit, and again, according to some, he did. A third, or it may have been the second, to avoid a similar impulse, and when actually about to use his razor, jumped through the window into Rhetoric Yard. He broke some bones, but saved his life. Subsequently no student could be induced to use the room, but a priest volunteered to sleep or keep vigil there for one night. In the morning, his hair was white, though no one dares to relate what his harrowing experiences might have been. Afterwards the front wall of the room was removed and a small altar of St Joseph was erected.

'The basic details of the story have doubtless some foundation in fact, and it is safe to assume that something very unpleasant did occur. The suicide (or suicides), in so far as one can deduce from the oral tradition that remains, seem to have taken place in the period 1842–48. A few colourful adjuncts that used to form part of the stock in trade of the story-teller are passing out of memory now. Modern students for instance do not point out the footprint burned in the wood, or the blood marks on the walls.'

THE EVIL EYE

A Happening on Aran

For those who believed in ghosts and spirits, it was the worst piece of luck to have some compliment paid to them, or a loved one, without some kind of action to pacify a malevolent spirit who might overhear. This was especially true if the person making the comment had a reputation for having the evil eye. To spit after making or hearing such a remark, or to immediately utter a blessing, helped to avert a reaction, but sometimes it was not possible. An Aran islander, Patrick Madden, recorded this:

'I'll tell you how I lost the first son I had. He was just three years old and as fine and strong as any child you'd see. And one day my wife said she'd bring the child to her mother's house to stop the evening with her, for I was going out. And there was a neighbour of ours, a man that lived near us, and no one was the better of being spoken to by him. And as they were passing his house, he came out, and he said, "That's the finest child that's in the island." And a woman that was passing at the same time stopped and said, "It was the smallest that ever I saw the day it was born, God bless it." And the mother knew what she meant, and she wanted to say "God bless him," but it was like as if a hand took and held her throat, and choked her that she couldn't say the words. And when I came to the mother's house, and began to make fun

73

with the child, I saw a round mark on the side of his head, the size of a crown piece. And I said to the wife, "Why would you beat the child in the head, why don't you get a little rod to beat him if he wants it?" And she said that she had never touched him at all.

'And at that time, I was very much given to playing cards, and that night I went out to a friend's house to play. And the wife before she went to bed broiled a bit of fish and put it on a plate with potatoes, and put it in a box in the room, for fear it might be touched by a cat or a rat or such like. But I was late coming in and didn't mind to eat it. And the next night I was out again. And when we were playing cards we'd play first with tobacco and we'd go on to tea, and we'd end up with whiskey.

'And the next morning, when the wife opened the door, she laughed and she said, "You didn't drink your tea when you were out last night, for I see you have your dinner eaten."

'And I said, "Why should you say that? I never touched it." And she held up the plate and showed me that the potatoes were taken off it, but the fish wasn't touched, for it was a bit of a herring and salty.

'Well, the child was getting sick all the day, and I didn't go out that evening. And in the night, we could hear the noise as if of scores of rats, going about the room. And every now and again I struck a light, but as soon as the light was in it we'd hear nothing. But the noise would begin again as soon as it was dark, and sometimes it would seem as if they came up on the bed, and I could feel the weight of them on my chest as if they would smother me.

'And in the morning I chanced to open the box where the dinner used to be, and it as big a box as any in Aran, and, when I opened it, I saw it was all full of blood, up the sides and to the top, that you couldn't put your hand in it without getting bloody. I said nothing but shut the lid down again. But after, when I came into the house, I saw the wife rubbing at it with a thing called a flannel they got at Killinny.

'I asked her what she was doing, and she said, "I'm cleaning the box, where it's full of blood." And after that I gave up the child and I had no more hope for its life. But if they had told me that about the neighbour speaking to him, I'd have gone over, and I'd have killed him with my stick, but I'd have made him come and spit on him. After that we didn't hear the noise the same again, but we heard like the sound of a clock all through the night and every night. And the child got a swelling under the feet, and he couldn't put a foot to the ground. But that made little difference to him, for he didn't hold out a week.'

FLOATING ISLANDS

The Ballycotton Vision

On Sunday afternoon, 7 July 1878, the inhabitants of Ballycotton, a fishing harbour on the coast of County Cork, were surprised and excited to see, far out towards the horizon, an island where no island had previously existed. The Ballycotton fishermen knew the spot as one of their best fishing-grounds. Those with keenest eyes or glasses could see that the island was partly rocky and partly wooded; rising steeply from the sea at one end and sloping gently to the water at the other. It was not long before the bolder spirits manned their boats and set off for a closer look, followed by many others. Perhaps a hundred boats were in the water at the end of it, all heading out towards the island. But, as the first boats approached, the form of the island, so clearly seen from the shore, became dim and hazy. Its colours faded, and at last it vanished entirely in front of their eyes.

The floating island has been seen in many other locations along the coast. Not only the Cork coast, as at Ballydonegan Bay and Courtmacsherry, but further north, in Tralee Bay, and off the coast of Clare at Carrigaholt, and right up to Inishbofin, where it appeared as a mirror image to that island itself. What is this floating island? Some believe it to be an island of the Sithe, or fairy folk, who can direct it as they please, a sort of mobile out-station of Tir nan Og.

Another story is that the island was once rooted in the sea in Galway Bay, but the king of the island, a wicked man who ruled like a tyrant and kept a harem of more than a hundred queens, was at last abandoned by his people and his fate is to drift for evermore up and down the coast of Ireland, a lonely ghost who can never again find the solace of human company.

A Lucky Escape

In a Galway story, the floating island is said to be visible to some and not to others. One time, a fisherman managed to land on it. He saw a little house, and went in, and a nice-looking young woman came out of a room and said to him, 'What will you say to me?'

'You are a very nice lady,' he replied.

And a second and a third came, and asked him the same question, and he gave them the same answer. And then they said to him, 'You'd best run for your life.'

So he ran, and his curragh was still floating by the island, so he got in, and as he was paddling away, the island vanished.

The Island 'Caught'

Geraldus Cambrensis, Gerald the Welshman, who wrote about Ireland in the eleventh century, claimed that shortly before his coming to Ireland, a phantom isle was discovered off the west coast. Some young men attempted to approach it, but when they drew near, it sank into the water. Next day, it reappeared and when the men again tried to approach it, it sank again, as if mocking their attempt. Then they took advice from an old man, who told them they should let fly an arrow, tipped with red-hot steel, against the island. On their third attempt, this they did, and on that day, the island did not sink, and they were able to land on it and live there.

HAUNTED CASTLES AND HOUSES

The Spirits of Renvyle

W. B. Yeats, the great Irish poet, who lived from 1856–1939, was a confirmed believer in spirits and in another world which in many ways controls the destiny of the world in which we live. At Renvyle House, in Connemara, owned by his friend Oliver St John Gogarty, he is said to have conjured up the ghost of a previous resident, a teenage boy named Harold Blake who had performed the difficult feat of suicide by self-strangulation. Yeats's wife, known as George, had greater psychic powers than her husband, and she saw the boy's figure: which she described as 'pale-faced, red-haired, about fourteen years of age, standing by a pillar in the north room.' But this was not the only ghost of Renvyle. Mrs Yeats also saw a man's face at her upper-floor window. Renvyle was burnt down in the Civil War, but was handsomely rebuilt and used more recently as a hotel, but definitely one with atmosphere.

Yeats was said to have been able to communicate with the ghost of Renvyle, and to make it promise to not behave in a frightening way, especially to children and women. He himself had no fears about spirit-contact. On another occasion, staying with his friend, the staunchly traditionalist Catholic, Edward Martyn, at his castle in Clare, Yeats outraged his host by making invocations to the spirits from the room above Martyn's private chapel. To Martyn, Yeats was dabbling in black magic and toying with evil spirits, to the danger of his own soul.

In August 1952, a hotel manager was sleeping in the room at Renvyle believed to be Yeats's séance room, when he heard, in the darkness, an urgent clicking sound right by his ear, as if someone was snapping their fingers. He put the blanket over his head and eventually went to sleep.

The Ghosts of Wilton Castle

Wilton Castle, in southeastern Ireland, was destroyed by fire during the War of Independence. It had been the home of the Anglo-Irish Alcock family since the seventeenth century. It had a famous ghost in the form of Harry Alcock, head of the family, who died in 1840. On the anniversary of his death, it was said that he could be seen at sunset, driving slowly away from the castle gate in a ghostly carriage. Crowds would gather to watch out for the spectacle. A local blacksmith even claimed to have talked to the landlord's spectre.

Another unquiet spirit inhabited the same neighbourhood, that of Archibald Jacob, a friend of the Alcocks. In the uprising of 1798, Jacob was prominent among those who tortured anyone thought to have information about the rebellion. He died in 1836, by a fall from his horse, and his ghost haunted the roadside, liable to terrify late-night passers-by. On one occasion, when a priest was called to the castle to carry out an exorcism, the figure of Jacob was seen to appear in the fireplace, then vanish again in a cloud of smoke.

The Ghost of Castletown House

Castletown House at Celbridge, County Kildare, was built by William Connolly, Speaker of the Irish Parliament, in 1722. The house was inherited by his nephew, who married Lady Anne Wentworth, daughter of the Earl of Stafford. It was she who one day saw the figure of a tall man standing in the upper gallery, who proceeded to walk down a non-existent staircase, past a big window, taking little steps as though each stair was quite shallow. It paused and laughed, a high, cold, arrogant laugh, as though it were the rightful owner of the place, mocking at the people who lived there.

Ten years later, a staircase was built in exactly the location in which Lady Anne had seen the figure. More than twenty years after that, Lady Anne's son, Thomas Connolly, now the owner of the house, was walking in the garden with his wife, and recalling the strange story of what his mother had seen in the hall. A few days after that, he was out riding with the Kildare Hounds, and a wild and stormy November day it was. Many of the hunt gave up and went home, for the fox was proving to be tricky and elusive. Only Connolly and a handful of others were left, when Connolly noticed that a newcomer seemed to have joined them. Mounted on a fine black horse that looked as fresh as if it had just come out of the stable door, he was a long, tall fellow, dressed in grey, with great thigh-boots.

'Good day to ye,' called out Connolly. 'A poor day for sport, though.'

The man merely grinned, showing large, discoloured teeth, then set his horse to the slope of the hill and went galloping up. At that same moment, the hounds began to bay, as if they were closing in on their prey. Connolly followed the other horseman up the hill, but when he got to the brink, he reined in, astonished. The hounds were not to be seen, but the stranger stood there, dismounted from his horse, and with the bloody carcass of the fox held in both hands high above his head. He grinned again at Connolly, then lowered the fox's body to the level of his mouth, and in one swift bite with his great teeth, cut away the brush. Dropping the carcass he held it out to Connolly, still grinning.

The young squire of Castletown turned away in disgust, but the man then spoke.

'Connolly, if you will not take the brush, will you offer me a cup of something hot in your great house?'

The Connollys had always maintained a tradition of hospitality, and Thomas did not refuse, though there was something about the man, his leering smile, and his high voice, that turned his blood.

'There is hot rum punch at my house for all who want it,' he said.

The stranger entered the house at Connolly's side, and Connolly saw him pause and survey the great entrance hall, and the staircase that came sweeping down from the gallery, past the window, and he heard a sound of hissing laughter from the man's lips. The stranger took a chair by the fire, and stretched out his legs as the other huntsmen were doing, but when a servant came up, to help take his riding boots off, he waved the man away.

'Leave me be,' he said. 'I am sleepy and don't choose to be disturbed.'

He closed his eyes and appeared to settle down for a comfortable nap. Coming more closely to get a good look at him, Connolly was amazed to see that the stranger was as hairy as an animal. Coils of hair matted on the backs of his hands and more emerged at his cuffs. Tufts of coarse hair sprang from his ears. Beginning to have suspicions, Connolly told two of the servants to take off one of the sleeping stranger's boots. As they cautiously worked it off, a thickly haired leg appeared, terminating in a great black hairy hoof.

Hastily, as all the company retreated from the fire, Connolly sent a man to ride for the parish priest. As the priest arrived, the stranger awoke, glanced at his feet and saw one boot had been removed. With a snarl he rose up, and placed himself against the mantelpiece, right in front of the roaring fire, and laughed the same high-pitched, spine-chilling laugh that Lady Anne had heard all those years ago in the same room. The priest, as terrified as anyone, mumbled an incantation, but it had no effect except to provoke further demoniac laughter. At last, the priest in desperation threw his missal at the figure. It missed its target and struck the mirror above the fireplace, which shattered. But, at the threat of being touched by the holy book, the figure leapt high in the air and vanished, leaving only a greasy boot in the room, and a great crack in the stone fireplace.

The Woman of Waterford

In 1999, it was reported that a family in the Grange area of Waterford had been haunted for twenty years by the ghost of a woman. Said to be usually a 'nice' ghost, it had the form of a middle-aged woman, with dark hair tied back in a bun, and her habitual place was on the stairs of the house, where she could keep a watch on the family's comings and goings. She spoke to the children, who did not experience fear. There was some poltergeist-type activity associated with her – cutlery might suddenly bend, or there would be gentle tappings in the wall. The only person who found the presence threatening was the children's mother, who felt that the ghost was hostile to her, and indeed on one occasion it tipped her out of her chair.

The Ghost of Lady Clanbrassil

In the middle of the seventeenth century, when Oliver Cromwell was making his notorious way through Ireland, he met an unexpected check at Killyleagh Castle on the shore of Strangford Lough. This was the home of the First Earl of Clanbrassil, a supporter of King Charles I in the civil war against the London

Parliament. The Earl had raised a force to try to relieve Carrickfergus Castle, held by the Roundheads, but his effort failed. His little army scattered and all had to flee to find safety where they could. Clanbrassil could not get back to Killyleagh. At that time, it was little changed from the old Norman keep and court-yard that had been built in the twelfth century. The Earl's wife, Anne, summoned all his tenants and retainers, brought them into the castle, and issued them with weapons. The gates were barred, ready to withstand the inevitable siege. Soon enough, the Cromwellians arrived.

A castle commanded by a woman should have been no great problem for such seasoned troops. But they were forced back by the determination of the defend-ers. They returned and tried to batter down the great wooden doorway. But the Earl's wife had seen to it that the gate was solidly reinforced from behind. When the soldiers attempted once again to storm the walls, every manner of missile from arrows to kitchen furniture forced them back once again. It was only when food supplies ran out and her faithful garrison was beginning to starve, that a signal offering truce was sent out. It was accepted by the besiegers. The makeshift garrison was allowed to make an honour-able exit from the castle, led by its commander. Cromwell imposed a fine of £10,000 on Clanbrassil, but the lady, by ardent pleading, got him to reduce it by half. Not only that, she obtained a pardon for her husband.

Killyleagh, still standing above an inlet of the lough,

was much altered and rebuilt in the mid-nineteenth century. But its great hall is still said to be patrolled by the figure of a woman in seventeenth-century costume. No one who knows the history of the place doubts that this is Anne, Countess of Clanbrassil, whose spirit still defends the castle she so bravely held against the might of Oliver Cromwell.

The Ghost Servants of Dunluce

The ruins of Dunluce Castle are set picturesquely on a crag above the sea on the Antrim coast, separated by a deep cleft from the mainland, and reached by a narrow bridge. The position is literally above the sea, since beneath the castle rock is a cave, directly open to the sea – a handy route for access or escape in times of trouble, and Dunluce was often involved in both. It has been a fortified site since early times, but most of what can be seen today was built by Sorley Boy ('Yellow Sorley') McDonnell in the sixteenth century. Close by, the Armada ship, *Girona*, was wrecked in 1588, and some of its cannons were salvaged and mounted in the castle.

Apart from the toll of sieges, Dunluce suffered a natural disaster, when on a night in 1639, part of the rock facing the sea collapsed, taking some of the castle buildings, (principally the kitchens and storerooms) with it. Many servants were busy in these rooms when the disaster happened. There was no warning, and many were drowned, or crushed by falling rock and masonry. The kitchens and storerooms were rebuilt, but visitors to the castle, particularly at twilight, have sometimes heard cries and sounds of lamentation, coming not from within the castle precinct, but from *beyond the present edge of the rock.* Although these have been dismissed as wind effects, they have also been noted at times when there was no wind, and a calm sea. After 1642, the McDonnells no longer lived in Dunluce Castle, and it fell into decay and ruin.

Earl Richard's Ghost

Dunluce Castle, on its rocky site on the Antrim coast, is also associated with Richard de Burgh, Earl of Antrim, in the fourteenth century when the Scots dynasty of Bruce were seeking to make themselves Kings of Ireland. Earl Richard's ghost is said to walk the castle on stormy nights.

The Spirit of Greencastle

Another legend links the son of Earl Richard, Earl William de Burgh, with Greencastle, by the shore of Lough Foyle. Earl William had a daughter, who had been out walking along the shore below Benvenagh when she was caught in a quicksand. Her life was saved by the son of Sir Walter Burk. The young pair fell in love. But unfortunately the Burks and the de Burghs were on opposite sides, as Sir Walter was allied to the O'Donnells who were at war with Earl. William. When the young man was captured, the Earl showed him no mercy and shut him up in a tower to starve to death. When his daughter was found bearing food to her beloved, he caught her by her long hair and threw her from the battlements to her death.

Greencastle has long been a ruin, but a ruin haunted by the figures of a young man and a young woman, still mourning their tragic love affair.

The Antrim Castle Noises

Originally built in the seventeenth century, Antrim Castle was twice burned down. The first time was in 1816, after which it was rebuilt. But, since its destruction in 1933, it has, like many other castles and country houses, remained a roofless ruin. Since then, many people have reported hearing sounds coming from the derelict building, described as being like slow, heavy breathing. But nothing has been found to identify the cause.

The 'Little Old Lady'

At Ballyalla House, near Ennis, a figure described as a 'little old lady' sometimes appears. Her history is not known, but a favourite place of hers is the main staircase, where many visitors have seen her.

The Hanged Man

At Erribal House, Labasheeda, County Clare, the terrifying figure of a hanged man used to appear, his head wrested violently to one side by the rope. It was the ghost of a man called Letherly, who had been hanged for murder early in the nineteenth century. A member of the Power family, who lived in the house, had sat on the jury which condemned him. Late in the century, the house was exorcized, in order to rid it of the baleful spectre.

The Spirits of Leap Castle

Leap Castle, an old fortress of the O'Carrolls near Birr in County Offaly, has been described as one of the most haunted castles in the country.

One man sleeping there woke feeling a strange, chill feeling at his heart, though the room was not cold. At the foot of his bed, he saw the tall form of a woman, clothed in red, her right hand raised. He reached for his matchbox and lit a match, and as he did so, the figure vanished.

Much more horrifying was the experience of the lady of the castle. She was in the gallery that runs above the great hall on one side, leaning over the balustrade, when she felt two hands laid on her shoulders. At the same time, there was a sickening stench of decay. Turning round, she saw that right behind her was a human-shaped creature, though hardly more than four feet high, with two black holes for eyes. Though the hands on her shoulders had felt bony, its body seemed soft, and from it came the awful deathly smell. Even as she gazed horrorstruck at it, the thing disappeared, and the smell with it.

Sometimes the figures of a little old man and woman have been seen, dressed in a style that suggests servants of an earlier period; he in cutaway jacket, breeches and buckled shoes; she in a green gown. Elsewhere in the castle there is an extension known as the Priest's House, and a figure cowled like a monk has been seen to walk out through the window of a room here.

Like many castles, Leap has a legend of hidden

treasure, in this case said to have been hoarded by one of the O'Carrolls in the fifteenth century. Summoned to Dublin to answer a charge of rebellion, he buried his treasure before leaving, but, on his return from imprisonment in Dublin Castle, he could not remember where he had hidden it. He went mad in his fruitless search for it. Nor has anyone ever discovered it.

One visitor to the castle, a lady with psychic powers, suddenly stopped in a corridor and said, 'I can sense that there is something here, though what it is I cannot say.'

When the wall was broken open, a tiny chamber with two skeletons in it was discovered, but no sign of gold or treasure.

Derrygonelly Farmhouse

The farmhouse at Derrygonelly was a typical farmhouse of the later nineteenth century, with a living room and two smaller rooms off it, which were used as bedrooms. And, of course, with no electric light. It was situated near Enniskillen, County Fermanagh, and occupied by a family of six, which included the widowed farmer, his son, and four daughters.

The eldest child was one of the girls, Maggie. She was almost twenty at the time that the hauntings began, and it seems that they had some connection with her. Unlike the great majority of rural cases, this one came to the attention of some high-powered ghost-watchers, including Sir William Barrett, a former President of the Society for Psychical

Research (the SPR) and also a distinguished scientist and Fellow of the Royal Society. The first signs were noises – rapping and scratching sounds that sometimes continued through the night. These were succeeded by moving objects. Some items were found right outside the cottage after thumps and bangs in the dark of the night. Lamps and candles seemed to be the especial objects of hatred of whatever was the source of the noises. It became impossible to keep any of these in the house overnight.

The farmer was a Methodist, and was advised to leave an open Bible in the room occupied by Maggie and her younger sisters, with its pages weighed down by stones. This had no effect and indeed the stones were removed and pages from the holy book torn out.

Sir William Barrett visited the cottage with Mr Thomas Plunkett from Enniskillen. His report, quoted by Peter Underwood in his *Gazetteer of Scottish and Irish Ghosts*, runs in part:

'After the children, except the boy, had gone to bed, Maggie lay down on the bed without undressing, so that her hands and feet could be observed. The rest of us sat round the kitchen fire, when faint raps, rapidly increasing in loudness, were heard coming apparently from the walls, the ceiling and various parts of the inner room, the door of which was open. On entering the bedroom with a light, the noises at first ceased but recommenced when I put the light on the windowsill in the kitchen-cum-living room. I had the boy and his father by my side, and asked Mr Plunkett to look round the house outside. Standing in the doorway leading to the affected bedroom, the noises recommenced; the light was gradually brought nearer, and after much patience I was able to bring the light into the bedroom while the disturbances were still loudly going on. At last I was able to go up to the side of the bed, with the lighted candle in my hand, and closely observed each of the occupants lying on the bed. The younger children were apparently asleep, and Maggie was motionless; nevertheless, knocks were going on everywhere around, on the chairs, the bedstead, the walls and the ceiling. The closest scrutiny failed to detect any movement on the part of those present that could account for the noises, which were accompanied by a scratching or tearing sound. Suddenly a large pebble fell in my presence on the bed; no one had moved to dislodge it, even if it had been placed for the purpose. When I replaced the candle on the windowsill of the kitchen, the knocks became still louder, like those made by a heavy carpenter's hammer driving nails into flooring.'

Barrett came three more times to the cottage on consecutive nights, with other members of the SPR, and each time the noises repeated themselves.

Prompted by the farmer, who said that the ghost in the house could answer questions by means of raps, Sir William tried the experiment of asking mentally for a certain number of raps to be done. Immediately, the ghost rapped to order. He repeated this four times, with the correct number of raps being made each time.

One of Barrett's companions, the Reverend

Maxwell Close, read some passages from the Bible, to the accompaniment at first of a terrific din. This gradually ceased, and by the time the minister came to recite the Lord's Prayer, things had calmed down. After that, the hauntings at Derrygonelly came to a stop.

Rahona Lodge

This house at Carrigaholt, County Clare, was the summer home of the Keane family. Charlotte Keane wrote in 1917 of the presence of a ghost in 'the little dark room facing west'. 'Lucky ghost,' she went on, thinking about the remoteness of the house, 'it can come when it likes.' There was definitely something eerie about the house and the locals would never come by there after nightfall.

The Ghosts of Glenarm

Glenarm Castle, in County Antrim, was one of the seats of the McDonnell family. The artist Hector McDonnell grew up there. He recalls it as being just about as thoroughly haunted as a place could be. But the family did not allow itself to be fazed by the phantom residents with whom they shared the castle; they felt it was somehow the right and inevitable thing that a family with such a long and often violent history should have a few ghosts. 'Ghosts lend social éclat to a place,' said Hector McDonnell, implying that if you don't have a few around then you can't be out of the top drawer.

His mother, however, had every room in the castle

exorcized, except the attic. The ghosts retreated to the attic, from where loud noises of stamping and moaning could be heard. As an intrepid boy of twelve, Hector remembers going up the attic stairs to investigate. But as he went up, the light, which he had turned on at the foot of the staircase, was put out. With a numbing sensation, he realized that whoever or whatever had done that was now behind him. Mastering his terror, he somehow got down again. For fifteen years, the attic remained undisturbed.

Ross House

This country house above Clew Bay has its full share of ghostly activity. Among the ghosts who have appeared in the house, a former maidservant has been identified – seen both in a bedroom and on the stairs. Footsteps have been heard going up and down a staircase that no longer exists. Figures have been seen seated before the fire in the drawing room, and one man testified to having see a 'terrible face' at the window of the drawing room.

The 'Ape Ghost'

The Reverend John Seymour recounts the experience of an American family, father, mother, daughter and son, who rented an old castle in one of the southern counties. Pleased to get it at a low rental, they did not give credence to tales of ghosts and hauntings there, and even when the servants complained about strange noises, they put it down to over-imagination.

However, one night, while her husband was away,

the lady heard similar noises to those described by the servants. She was in her bedroom, when she heard a door closed with a bang, then the sound of stealthy, shuffling footsteps in the corridor outside her room. Taking a lighted candle, she opened the door to look outside. At the far end of the corridor she saw a figure moving with a shambling tread towards the staircase. She raised the light to get a better view, and at that point the figure turned, and she saw a human face, but one of great hideousness, on top of what appeared to be an ape's body. The thing abruptly disappeared. She shrieked with horror, and ran back into her room. Her daughter tried to persuade her that it was a bad dream, and she said nothing to her husband about it when he returned.

He, however, had his own encounter with the thing, when, a few nights later, at the end of the evening, he was coming up the stairs in the great entrance hall, and suddenly heard weird and unpleasant laughter. As he looked up to the landing above him, he saw the thing looking down at him – it had the face of a man of about forty, deathly white, hairless, and distorted by an expression of malevolent glee. The body was like that of a great ape, thickly clad in reddish hair, and the creature, as it gripped the balustrade, appeared to be shaking with laughter. The man rushed up the stairs towards it, upon which, whilst uttering peals of diabolical laughter, it vanished. Hearing the sound of laughter, the other members of the family came out of their rooms, and he told them what he had seen. His wife then told her story. They then searched all the rooms, but found nothing in any way untoward in any of them.

This mettlesome family decided to stay on and see if they could get to the bottom of the mystery, but for some time there were no sightings of the creature, only occasional nocturnal sounds: footsteps, groans, slamming doors. But one afternoon, in broad daylight, while the lady was in the drawing room arranging flowers at a table, she felt a slight noise behind her, and two hands were laid lightly on her shoulders. Thinking it was the friend, who was staying with them at this time, she turned round, saying, 'Oh, there you are,' and found herself looking right into the face of the malignant apparition of the night. It stood there, fully six feet high, chuckling with a kind of horrid glee. She saw the pale, hairless face, with gleaming red eyes, and the thick matting of hair that covered the body, screamed, and fainted. Just then, her friend came into the room, in time to see the figure before it vanished.

After this, the family left the castle, and the further history of the ghost-beast, which in description somewhat resembles an orang-utan, is not recorded.

'Lady Reid's' House

'Lady Reid' is the presiding spirit in one of the tall town houses in Fitzwilliam Square, Dublin. She has been held responsible for strange noises, also for the disappearance or movement of various objects in the house. One of those who encountered Lady Reid was the Scottish romantic novelist Annie S. Swan (Mrs

Burnett Smith in her private life) who visited the house on a number of occasions. On one occasion she was sharing her hostess's bedroom, when she was wakened in the middle of the night by a dreadful-sounding, rattling, clashing noise. It was made by a Venetian blind that appeared to have pulled up all by itself. The unsurprised lady of the house merely commented, 'Oh, it's Lady Reid', and went back to sleep. Indeed, that particular family – rather unusually – seemed to rather cherish their resident ghost, despite her terrorising effect both on visitors and on the servants. Whether because of the associations of the room itself, or because she had a prejudice against visitors, it seemed to be the guest room that was most haunted by Lady Reid. The servants would only enter it two at a time. The doughty Annie S. Swan apparently made repeated visits, but many guests must have left saying to themselves, 'Never again.'

The Tragedy at Skryne Castle

In *More Ghosts in Irish Houses*, Michael Reynolds tells the story of events at this castle not far from the River Boyne, for long the home of the Palmerston family. In 1740, the house was lived in by Sir Bromley Casway, and his ward, Lilith Palmerston, a girl of great beauty, but who was shy and retiring by nature. Not far from Skryne lived another country landowner, Phelim Sellers. Sellers was a widower, but there were stories that his wife had died as a result of his ill-treatment. He was a hard-riding, hard-drinking, foul-mouthed character, who came to Skryne to play cards with Sir Bromley, but who was clearly interested in the girl. On one occasion, in the grounds, he made an approach to her, which was rejected; and only the intervention of one of the castle gardeners prevented him from attacking her. Lilith Palmerston wanted to leave Skryne for Dublin, where her guardian had a town house, to get away from Sellers, and Sir Bromley agreed. But on the eve of their departure, Sellers broke into Skryne Castle, entered Lilith's room, and killed her by thrusting foxglove fronds down her throat. He then fled, but was ultimately caught, and hanged for the crime.

Visitors and residents of Skryne have heard screams in the night from no obvious source; and some have seen the figure of a woman in white, clutching at her throat, running from the house. Others have told of a big man, with a hard hat, and a stick, with a dog beside him.

Michael Cleary's House

In July 1895, a strange murder trial was held. The accused, Michael Cleary, aided and abetted by a 'fairy doctor' – a man supposed to have skills in identifying and dealing with changelings – had burnt his wife Bridget to death, in their home in the town of Ballyvadlea, County Tipperary.

Cleary had been persuaded that his wife, who had been ill, was actually possessed by a fairy spirit. The tests and torments she was subjected to were justified by the fact that this was how the changeling spirit was forced out of the human body and back to its own place. At this point, the human spirit would be able to return.

After his wife's death, and before he was arrested, Cleary spent three nights by the edge of a fairy rath on Kylenagranagh Hill, near to his house, waiting, with a black-handled knife held ready in his hand, for his wife to appear on a grey horse. As she did so, he was to sever the bridle-rein and free her. But Bridget Cleary did not appear. After five days, Michael Cleary was arrested and duly sentenced to life imprisonment for her murder, after a trial whose details astonished the country and indeed the world.

One strange aspect of the whole story is that the house in which these events took place was itself built on the site of what was reputed to be a fairy rath. Although the Clearys were apparently unaware of it, previous tenants had been disturbed by strange sounds at night, and had eventually left the place because of this. It has always been held as most inadvisable to disturb these places; and to build on one is to invite repercussions. Many people have speculated on a possible link between this and the strange obsession that seized Michael Cleary and his relatives – including the victim's own father.

The White Lady of Kinsale

The military fort at Kinsale was begun in 1677, and reinforced and extended several times afterwards. From quite an early stage in its history, the story of the 'White Lady' has been associated with it. Accounts of the precise circumstances in which she met her end vary, but the common factor is the suicide of a young bride on the very day of her wedding. Her father was the colonel in charge of the fort, named as either Warrender or Browne, a strict disciplinarian with a violent temper. The girl, whose name has been handed down as the rather curious 'Wilful', was engaged to a young officer, Sir Trevor Ashurst. On the evening of their marriage, they were strolling along the battlements, which rise above the cliffs. Looking over the wall by one of the sentry-posts, she saw some wild flowers growing, and said she would like to have them. To please the new bride, the sentry volunteered to climb down and pick the flowers; and Sir Trevor jovially said he would take the sentry's musket and stand guard while he was gone.

The evening was getting chilly, and Wilful went inside. The sentry seemed to take a long time to return with his nosegay. Sir Trevor, tired and none too serious about his sentry-role, sat in the sentry-box and dozed off to sleep. The soldier never came back – perhaps he had never planned to; perhaps he fell to his death on the crags. When the stern colonel came round inspecting the sentry-posts, he only saw a sleeping man inside. Enraged, he drew his pistol and fired, with the intention of scaring the fellow awake. But, in his haste, he failed to aim away and the bullet passed through the heart of his new son-in-law.

When the bride learned what had been brought about by her casual wish, she rushed out and threw herself off the battlements. The colonel, distracted by guilt and grief, shot himself that night. Such is the burden of one day's tragic happenings.

In the years around 1820, the officer in charge of the fort was Major Black. One summer evening, he saw the figure of a young woman dressed in white appear at the doorway of his own quarters and go up the stairs. Thinking at first it was a lady who had come in by the wrong door, he moved to speak to her, but something held him back. He saw how noiselessly she moved; and then noticed how old-fashioned her clothes were. The major followed the lady upstairs and saw her enter one of the bedrooms; but when he knocked and entered, the room was empty. The White Lady was also seen in Major Black's quarters by the little daughter of a soldier. Black's friend, Dr Craig, related these sightings in his book, *Real Pictures of Clerical Life in Ireland*.

These manifestations caused no fear or injury, but later in the nineteenth century, more violent events were reported. An army doctor, returning to his rooms from an afternoon's snipe-shooting, was stooping to pick up his key when he felt himself being dragged along the hall by an unseen force and pitched bodily down a flight of steps. He was knocked out, but remembered that as he fell, he had caught sight of a figure in white, which reminded him of a woman in a wedding dress.

Another officer, Captain Jarvis, had a similar experience a little later. He too had a glimpse of a white figure vanishing away as he approached his door. He could not get it to open, and when he tried to force it, he felt a powerful cold gust, and he too was thrown down the flight of stairs.

The White Lady is still said to walk, especially on calm summer evenings, like the one on which her life came to its sudden and tragic end.

The Haunted Rectory

The rectory at Carlingford was built in the seventeenth century and was first occupied by the Stannus family, one of whom, an ancestor of Dame Ninette de Valois, the famous ballerina, extended the house. It was bought around the year 1870 by the Church of Ireland to use as the local rector's house. In 1960, it was a twenty-two room house, and had just been bought from the Church by the painter Ernest McDowell. In 1963, it was still empty.

About five o' clock one hot evening in early September, both Ernest McDowell and his brother were by the house, McDowell mowing the lawn and his brother cutting corn in a nearby field. Looking up, McDowell saw the figure of a girl in a red velvet dress moving towards the door. Before he could see her face, she disappeared. He identified the dress as belonging to the Edwardian period. Looking around him, McDowell now saw another figure – coming in at the gate was a clergyman, wearing a high, stiff collar. Even as McDowell looked at him, the figure vanished. He was convinced that there was some link between the two.

The rectory had some earlier records of strange happenings. A previous resident, Canon Meissner, had also seen the girl in the red dress, on this occasion inside the house. The canon's wife and daughter had both heard footsteps on the back stairs when no one else was in the house to make them; and his daughter had also once observed one of the dining room doors vibrate, as if under pressure, and then burst open, and though apparently no one entered, her dog stared, raised its hackles, and finally fled away. Ernest McDowell was sensitive to psychic manifestations, and he too had heard footsteps. Although he felt sure there were presences in the house, they did not seem to him to be unhappy or disturbing ones.

The ghost hunter, Hans Holzer, took an interest in the house, and went to visit Canon Meissner and his family in 1965. They had lived in the rectory for twenty-five years up to 1960, and had noticed a number of odd things. Mrs Meissner had been told that the ghost of a sea captain, drowned at sea, had come back to the house, his original home; and on some summer evenings, she would feel the presence of something white and silent going by. On one occasion, when they had been visited by the sister of Ninette de Valois, a young man staying in the house as a guest had declared her to be the exact image of a ghostly figure he had seen in the guest room. Strangely, too, on being shown round the house, she had felt that she had been in the guest room before, although it was her first visit to Carlingford Rectory.

The spectral sea captain was never tracked down, but the researches of Holzer, who also used the services of a medium, Sybil Leek, to communicate with the spirit of the girl in the red dress, and of McDowell, convinced them that there had been some kind of romantic tragedy in the house during the mid-nineteenth century, involving the girl and the clergyman, which kept their restless spirits still on the site.

The Ghost of Howth Castle

Elsewhere in this book you will find the story of the rat of Howth Castle. But that is not only the only ghostly presence to haunt the building.

The robust military figure of Lieutenant-Colonel Cyril Foley, soldier and author, was invited for a weekend's shooting by Lord Howth, just around the start of the twentieth century. When Foley heard that the castle had a wing believed to be haunted, he immediately wanted to sleep there and test it out. This part of the castle had been unused and locked, but a bed was made up for him in a little tower room, with narrow mullioned windows and a big stone fireplace. It was reached by a spiral stone staircase. The only lighting was provided by candles. As Foley was dressing for dinner, on a calm and windless evening, the candles suddenly sputtered and went out. He found matches, relit them, and again they went out. For a second time, he relit them, and yet again, after a moment or two, they went out. The curtains were closed and the room was pitch dark. Foley began to walk towards the door, when he heard light footsteps on the wooden floor behind him. Opening the door, he went on down the stairs, still hearing the noise of footsteps following. As he drew nearer the inhabited part of the house, Foley broke into a run, and was appalled to hear the footsteps behind him do the same. At last, Foley reached the door of a fellow-guest's room, and burst in unceremoniously, tie undone, his trouser braces undone, and in a panic most uncharacteristic of an experienced soldier. He resolved to take hauntings more seriously in future.

The Shallardstown Carriage

James Reynolds, who investigated strange events in many of Ireland's country houses, recounted the macabre story of Shallardstown, a great Palladian house built in County Tipperary by Cadogan Parrott, early in the nineteenth century. He had married Angelica Gammage, but she killed herself, while of unsound mind, leaving him with two daughters, Angelica and Rosaleen. Angelica became her father's hostess, and, as he died soon after, found herself mistress of the house. She had chosen a husband for herself in the handsome but impoverished Dagan Ferritter. But Ferritter ran away with, and married, her sister Rosaleen. Despite her bitter resentment at being passed over, she paid the couple a small regular allowance.

Angelica, herself, made a distinguished marriage with a Russian nobleman, Prince Nicholas Orloff, whom she met in London, where he was an attaché at the Russian Embassy. They married, and Shallardstown was shut up whilst they lived in St Petersburg and Paris. But, in 1838 Orloff died, and his wife, now a Princess, returned to her Irish estate. Here she led a secluded life, attended by a discreet and silent butler named Creed. She was never seen. But she had not forgotten the slight done her by Dagan Ferritter. He had turned out to be a gambler and had piled up considerable debts, which he hoped to repay as Angelica had intimated that she would leave her wealth to her sister, her only relative. The couple returned to Ireland, penniless except for Angelica's dole. The butler explained she was unwell and could not receive visitors. Yet every day at three o'clock, her fine landau would leave Shallardstown and take a drive through the countryside, and the Princess could be seen sitting up inside, holding a jewel-handled whip. Rosaleen and her husband settled in a cabin by the edge of the demesne, living on next to nothing, and waiting for their inheritance.

They waited for years, never admitted to the great house, until Ferritter, egged on by some of the pub drinkers of nearby Clogheen, one day went up and demanded to speak to the Princess. Impassive as ever, Creed told them that the Princess had in fact been dead for eleven years. On her instructions, her mummified corpse had been installed in the landau, whip in hand, and it was that which had been driven so regularly through the gates. She had left a letter dated 12 May 1861, explaining her intention. Practically overcome by the notion that for eleven years they had lived in misery for no reason, both Rosaleen and Dagan Ferritter did not live long to enjoy their inheritance.

In 1898, the house became a boys' school, and it

was at that time that accounts began of a purple-dressed figure in the hall, and the sound of the wheels of a departing carriage. By 1937, when Reynolds visited the place, it was empty and neglected but the caretaker told him that she had seen a figure at the top of the stairs, and heard footsteps go up and down. Hardly a trace now remains of the house.

The Tunnel at Queen's

Even in the sceptical modern surroundings of a university, there may be odd corners where strange presences are felt. Between two parts of the Queen's University complex in Belfast, the Ashby and David Keir wings, there is a tunnel for pedestrians. Even as such places go, it always seems colder and darker there than in other walkways. This is a long-inhabited part of the city. An early monastic settlement was nearby. Later, the Friars Bush Cemetery was established, one of the oldest in the city. Many people making their way between the two buildings shun the tunnel; some have spoken of feeling an 'intense, unnatural coldness' in going through it. On one occasion, three men went into the tunnel; two turned back, unbeknown to the man in the lead. He went on through, convinced all the way that he had a companion walking right behind him. But when he reached the end and looked back, he found he was alone.

The Ballyheigue Photograph

In June 1962, a military officer, Captain P. D. O'Donnell, on holiday in Kerry, took a stroll with his eight-year-old son up to the ruins of Ballyheigue Castle, on the coastal cliffs by the small fishing village of the same name. Like many others, the castle had been burned out in 1921. Captain O'Donnell had his camera, and took a few shots of the castle, including one of the little boy standing inside, against a wall that ran at right angles to the castle's façade, and caught in a shaft of sunlight from a window. When they returned home, and the film was developed, O'Donnell saw that there was a second figure in the photograph.

Although partly obscured by the sunlight coming through the window, it was clearly a male figure holding a sword and with its legs clad in leggings or tight-fitting boots. Certain that it was not a double exposure, and equally certain that there had been no one else present when the photograph was taken, he was mystified and even slightly alarmed.

He told various friends about it, and passed the print and negative around those who were most interested, in the course of which the envelope containing them disappeared 'most mysteriously', but not before more than a dozen reliable people had seen both. O'Donnell advertised in the hope of recovering the photograph, and was interviewed by one or two newspapers. Soon afterwards, he received offers to buy the evidence from Sweden and Denmark. Intrigued by this, he did some research into the history of the castle.

For long before its destruction in 1921, it had been the home of the Crosbies, a family who dominated that part of the North Kerry coast. On the night of 20

October 1730, a Danish ship, the *Golden Lyon,* was wrecked off that coast – some said lured in by misleading lights. Outward bound for the East Indies, the ship carried twelve chests of silver and coins. These were salvaged, and the crew rescued, by Sir Thomas Crosbie and his men. Whilst the question of salvage was being settled, the Danes, and their silver, remained at Ballyheigue Castle. In a very short time, Sir Thomas died.

Although rumour had it that he was poisoned by his wife Margaret, she claimed the then huge sum of £4,500 in damages for the salvage and his loss. The Danish Captain Heitman had the silver chests stored in the tower cellar, but in June 1731, the castle was stormed by a gang of fifty or sixty men. Though their faces were blackened, one of the Danes recognized a relative of Lady Margaret's. Two Danes died in the attack, another was wounded, and the silver chests were taken away. Heitman was in no doubt that the whole thing was a put-up job, with the lady at the bottom of it.

Although several men were brought to trial for their part in the raid, Lady Margaret steadfastly denied any knowledge of it. One man, clearly not a ringleader, was hanged; one who turned king's evidence was later found dead. About three quarters of the Danish treasure disappeared and was never recovered – reason enough perhaps for a Danish officer to linger in spirit about the place. O'Donnell also realized that his photograph was taken at almost exactly the time of year on which the raid had taken place.

The Happenings at Summerhill Street

In January 1966, strange things occurred at Summerhill Street, then a run-down part of Georgian Dublin. At a time when conservation of historic or aesthetically-appealing buildings was given little official attention, a demolition squad had moved in on the street. But the Dublin *Evening Press* reported on 14 January that:

'Six Dublin men are being terrified by strange happenings in a house at Summerhill Street. The men moved into the house, Number 118, just a week ago to demolish it, and since then work has been held up by a succession of strange events.

'Three of the men claim to have seen a ghost standing in one of the rooms, but on three different occasions. All three say they saw the strange figure clearly.

'The oldest member of the group, Mr William McGregor, fainted and had to be revived.

'Now the men refuse to work on different floors in the house – they will not work at all unless they are allowed to remain on the same floor, within sight of each other.'

William McGregor described the figure as a tall man, wearing a striped shirt or overall, with no collar. As it stood there, looking at him, he blessed himself and fainted away. Another man, Joseph Byrne, was struggling to prise out an old stove in the basement when he felt something behind him. At first when he looked around, he saw nothing. But when the feeling recurred, and he looked again, he saw a man, dressed in what he took to be a butcher's striped jacket, standing looking towards a window. Byrne called the others, but when they came, they could see nothing. The third eyewitness was Thomas Kearney, the foreman. He too saw the striped jacket or shirt, but he also saw that the man had a napkin or something similar round his neck, as if he were prepared for a haircut or a shave.

Stories emerged about a ghost that had once haunted the adjoining house, Number 117, before it had been pulled down. Mr McGregor believed he had seen the ghost of Patrick Conway, a butcher who had cut his own throat at Number 118 in 1863. Number 118 was pulled down in the end, and no further reports were heard.

The Donnybrook Ghosts

Another haunted site in the apparently prosaic surroundings of Dublin was a house in Donnybrook, Ballinguile, now pulled down and with an apartment block on its site. But the last family to live in it, the Healys, had a number of curious experiences. Footsteps were often heard, particularly on the stairs, in summer months, and usually in the daytime. Most of Mrs Healy's children were grown up and away, but her youngest son, a student, was still living at home. When he had friends in, his mother usually went to bed.

On one occasion, young Healy was downstairs with a friend, and about nine o'clock he said to his mother that they were going out. She then dozed off, and awoke to hear the sound of a noisy party going on downstairs. People were talking, laughing, moving about. Mrs Healy was annoyed, since she disliked such impromptu happenings, and almost went down to complain to her son, but did not. Then the noise dwindled away, and soon afterwards she heard the front door open, and her son came in. He had not been in the house at all – indeed no one but Mrs Healy had been in the house.

On another occasion, Mrs Healy's small grand-daughter was seen in the enclosed yard behind the house, apparently talking to someone. Her mother and grandmother asked her who she had been talking to, and she replied: 'The tall dark man', in quite a natural way, as though he were quite familiar to her. Mrs Healy and her family eventually moved, but shortly before they did, they were aroused about eleven o'clock one night by the door bell ringing. Two policemen were at the door. They explained that they had heard a lot of noise, suggesting that violence of some kind was taking place, and coming from the house. Yet those inside had not heard anything at all.

HAUNTED CHURCHES AND CHURCHYARDS

The Voices of St Michan's

St Michan's Church, in Church Street, Dublin, is famous for the 'charnel house' in its vaults, where the dry air has mummified the corpses. There are about thirty such bodies, and although the atmosphere is perfectly still, some visitors who have lingered for a while in the vault have reported hearing sounds of loud whispering, as in an agitated discussion or argument.

'The Phantom of Death'

A strange legend is attached to the churchyard at Eringle Truagh. The novelist William Carleton (1794–1869), author of *Fardorougha the Miser*, was familiar with the story, and wrote after a visit to the spot:

'I have been shown the grave of a young person about eighteen years of age, who was said about four months ago to have fallen victim to the phantom, and it is not more than ten weeks since a man in the same parish declared that he gave a promise and fatal kiss to the ghost and consequently looked upon himself as lost. He took a fever and was buried on the day appointed for the meeting, which was exactly a month from the time of contact with the spirit. Incredible as it may seem the friends of these two persons declared, at least those of the young man did, to myself that particulars of the meeting with the phantom were detailed repeatedly by the two persons without variation. There are several other cases of the same kind mentioned . . . '

'The spirit of the churchyard seemed able to take male or female form. It would appear to a solitary mourner, always as a handsome, but above all sympathetic-looking figure. It would talk softly, tenderly, to the grieving person, assuring them that their dead friend or relative was now in a far happier condition than before. With such consoling talk, they would sit down together in the porch of the church, or on the stone wall. Gradually the mourner would forget his or her grief and think only of the wonderful sympathy and irresistible attraction of the person beside them. The attraction would seem to be mutual, and soon there was intertwining of hands, kissing and caressing. When at last they knew they must go, inflamed by sudden love, the visitors to the churchyard would say, "When will I see you again?"

"We cannot meet for four weeks," would be the answer. "But let us pledge ourselves now, that in four weeks' time we will meet again, in this very place."

'Eagerly the pledge would be made. Looking back from beyond the churchyard gate, they would no longer see the figure. As the trance of its charm gradually wore off, a cold fear would rise inside them. They had made a pact with the phantom of death. For all that they, their friends, even the priest, could do, they felt their days were numbered. Within four weeks they would catch a mortal illness, or simply decline and fade, until the fatal appointment was kept, to the day, by their own funeral.'

The Coach of Timogue

The old churchyard at Timogue was an especially haunted place. Unexplained lurid light could be seen there at night, and people who dared to go, or strayed, close enough talked of strange moaning sounds and even of white-clothed shapes that moved among the ancient tombstones. The road that runs by this churchyard is one where the terrifying phantom coach (*see* 'The Death Coach' section on page 63) was seen. A farmer and his servant, returning from the fair at Ballynahill, came by the churchyard late one night, though it was a place people avoided if they could. As they came by it, a sudden light appeared, shedding a spectral glow on the crumbling, ivy-covered walls of the church and on the tombs, and at the same moment they heard wheels rumbling behind. Swinging round, they saw, approaching them at breakneck speed, a great black coach, with the same ghastly luminescence around it as had appeared in the churchyard. The racing horses were headless, the driver likewise. They shrank against the roadside and as the vehicle went rushing past, they caught a fleeting glimpse of a skeleton face that grinned out from the carriage window.

HAUNTED ISLANDS

The Skellig Ghosts

In his book,*Ghosts and Ghouls*, T. C. Lethbridge relates how he and a friend visited Skellig Michael in June 1929. There was no pier and they had to jump from their boat on to a rocky ledge. Lethbridge climbed up to the top of the island, to view the six 'bee-hive' huts and the ruined chapel. Noticing a patch of nettles growing on the steep slope, and guessing there was an old dump or midden worth investigating, he set out to scramble down towards it. But then he stopped.

'When I was about half-way down . . . I had a remarkable sensation. Somebody, I felt, was wanting to push me off the cliff.'

He went on a few feet, feeling increasingly alarmed, then stopped and climbed back up again, thoroughly ashamed of his fear. Back on top, he was walking down to the dip known as 'Christ's Saddle' when he suddenly thought of turning round, but before he could do so, he was thrown flat on his face. There was no wind, and he had not tripped or stumbled. Despite his friend's wish to sleep overnight on the Skellig, he insisted on returning to Valentia. Back on Valentia Island, they were chatting to the telegraph operator, who surprised them by asking, 'See anything of the ghost?'

It transpired that the previous winter a ship had

foundered off the Skelligs. As the lighthouse-keepers sat at their meal, the outer door opened, and they heard the sound of seaboots crossing the floor, passing through into their sleeping quarters. Since then, there had been continual disturbances in the lighthouse, slamming of doors, strange cries, thumps and bangs. Two of the keepers had fled.

Lethbridge had no explanation to offer. When he told the island's owner of his experience, the owner suggested that perhaps the original pagan spirits, who had possessed the island before the Celtic saints colonized it, had returned, to fill the 'vacuum' left by the good men.

POLTERGEISTS

The Irish Maid

Mary Carrick emigrated from Ireland to the USA in May 1867. Illiterate but bright, and in good health, she quickly found a job as housemaid with the Willis family. Mr H. A. Willis himself told the story in a report for the *Atlantic Monthly* of August 1868, which he titled 'A Remarkable Case of Physical Phenomena'.

After Mary Carrick had been six weeks in the Willis house, the kitchen bells began to ring at intervals through the day, even though no one was pulling the cords. The bells themselves were eleven feet up on the kitchen wall. When disconnected, they continued to ring, but only when Mary was in the room, or the room adjoining. The rings were violent, as if the bells were being tugged hard. Then came rappings, on doors, walls and windows close to where Mary was at work. She herself grew nervous and hysterical as a result of the happenings. She feared dismissal and pleaded with the Willises, 'Please don't send me away.'

She had no friends or contacts in the USA to turn to. Some local Spiritualists, hearing of the case, showed interest, but Willis, convinced there must be some rational physical cause, would not admit them to the house. The happenings grew more violent. Chairs were tipped over, crockery flew across the room, tables were lifted and tilted. A heavy stone washing slab rose up, fell back, and broke. Things came to a climax in August, with pails tipping and spilling, the washtub emptying itself, and heavy furniture turned over, while furious raps and bangs were heard on the wall. Mary was sent away for a rest, and peace returned to the household, but when she came back it all broke out again. On 12 September, Mary suffered a nervous collapse, and was taken away to a nearby asylum. She briefly returned to work for the Willises but preferred to go back to the asylum, where she worked as a maid for the rest of her life.

Willis's own explanation for the attacks was that in some way they involved electricity. When he put glass insulators under Mary's bed and the kitchen table, these remained still whilst other objects continued to move. But he could not establish what kind of process it was, nor could he explain how Mary herself became clairvoyant for the duration of the attacks.

The Poltergeist of Coonian

Another famous individual with an interest in ghosts and the paranormal was Sir Shane Leslie, born in Glaslough, County Monaghan, in 1885. A well-known author in his day, he wrote some good ghost stories. In his autobiography, *The Film of Memory*, he recounts a real experience in the family home at Glaslough, when he saw the apparition of his late uncle:

'I awoke at Glaslough two years after Uncle Moreton's death, and to my surprise I saw him standing in the room. I was completely in possession of my senses and could see every object. Uncle Moreton said very deliberately to me, "I don't mind what you have written about me, but Uncle Stee will mind very much." '

'Uncle Stee' was another relative, Colonel Stephen Frewen. Leslie had recently written a character sketch of him, under the heading 'Sublime Failures'.

But Leslie also kept what he called a 'Ghost Book': a record of actual supernatural occurrences either witnessed by himself or reported to him. The book contains a report on a poltergeist or troublesome spirit that haunted a house near Brookeborough in County Fermanagh.

Local rumour had it that an old man had been murdered in the house at one time. Certainly no one seemed to reside there for very long. The record for brevity was held by one family who stayed only one night before fleeing from the place. Leslie's account focuses on a family by the name of Murphy as the chief sufferers. At times, it seemed as if the poltergeist were making muffled noises from the ground beneath the house; at others they would hear snoring coming from a bedroom known to be empty. One member of the family was horrified, on entering a bedroom, to see what appeared to be a human shape huddled under the bedclothes, but when she called others to come, there was nothing there. But in their own bedrooms, they were liable to have the bedclothes pulled right off them. In a bizarre display of talent, the spirit could even tap out tunes on the piano.

The Murphys were brave enough to stand their ground for a long time. They attempted to have the poltergeist exorcized by three priests but this apparently had little effect. Eventually they gave up, emigrated to America, and left the poltergeist behind. What happened to the house and its unseen occupant after that is not known.

'Corney'

One Dublin poltergeist actually used to speak to the family whose house it inhabited. They referred to it, or him, as 'Corney', and he answered to the name. His voice was said to sound as if it came out of an empty barrel. The servants, who slept in the kitchen, were afraid of Corney and asked to sleep in the attic instead. However, the first time they slept in the attic room, the doors of its cupboard burst open and Corney said: 'Ha! Ha! You devils, I am here before you. I am not confined to any particular part of this house.' He was seen only twice, once by someone who apparently died of fright as a result, and once by a seven-year-old boy, who described the figure to his mother as that of a naked man, with a curl on his forehead, and 'a skin like a clothes-horse'.

Corney had a somewhat warped sense of humour: his first manifestation was by mimicking the sound of someone on crutches when one member of the household had to temporarily go on crutches with a sprained knee. He would not allow anything to be kept in one of the kitchen cupboards, tossing out whatever anyone tried to put in there.

On one occasion, he announced he was going to have 'company' that evening, and if the residents wanted any water out of the soft-water tank, they should draw it before going to bed, as he and his guests would be using it. Next morning, the water was a sooty black, and there were sooty prints on the bread and butter in the pantry. When a clergyman came to investigate him, the crafty Corney kept quiet, and on being asked later by the servants, 'Corney, why did you not speak?' he said, 'I could not speak while that good man was in the house.'

Corney made life so lively for the family that they resolved to leave the house and sell the remainder of their lease. But each time someone came to look over the house, his antics speedily drove them away, until at last the lady of the house appealed to him to stop troubling prospective buyers. Corney relented; in fact he said, 'You will be all right now, for I see a lady in black coming up to this house, and she will buy it.' Within half an hour, a widow had called and agreed to take over the lease, and the family thankfully left Corney behind.

REVENANTS

A Second Death

An old man died on one of the Aran Islands, and was duly buried after a wake was held. But after three days, they found a new baby in the cradle, that had been empty. They saw at once that the 'baby' had an old look on its face, and its face was long, not like a baby's. A wise woman who came to the house looked at the baby, and said:

'He won't be with you long. He had three deaths to die, and this is his second.'

The baby lived for six years, and then it died, and was no longer seen.

A Wandering Shade

Near Drumacoo a man was walking in the wood, when he came across an old woman, whom he had not seen before. There was something lost-looking about her, and, thinking her to be a country-woman who had lost her way, he said:

'Is there anything I can do for you?'

'There is,' said she.

'Come home with me, and tell me about it.'

'I can't do that,' said the old woman, 'but what you can do is this – tell my friends that I am in great trouble, for twenty times in my life I missed going to church, and now they must say twenty Masses for me, to deliver me. And another thing – there's some small debts I never paid, and these are helping to keep me in trouble.'

'What is your name?' asked the man, but she would not say, and presently she disappeared, and he knew she was a ghost.

As he went about the countryside he would tell this story, and one day, as he told it in a house not far away, his hostess remembered her. They had an old woman servant there, one of the Shannons, and when she died it had come out that she had some little debts here and there, that could not be paid, for she had left nothing at all. So then inquiries were made, and it was found out where she owed the few shillings, and the debts were paid, and the Masses said. Not long after that, the man saw the old woman again.

'God bless you now, for what you did for me,' she said, 'for now I'm at peace.'

And an old saying was remembered then, that when someone dies owing money, the weight of the soul is greater than the weight of the body, and it cannot get away, but wanders the earth until someone has the courage to question it.

Ghost in a Tree

It is said that when you a see a tree shaking, there is a ghost in it. And there is a woman of whom it was said that for seven years after her death, she was kept in a tree in Kinadyfe; and for seven years after that she was kept under the arch of a little stone bridge, with the cold water running by, and no shelter from wind, cold or frost.

At the end of the second seven years, the woman's husband came across the bridge, on his way home from Loughrea, and she rose to meet him. But he was terrified at the sight of her, and would not stop, but hurried on his way. That same evening, the woman appeared in the home of her own daughter, who fainted away when she saw her mother. But her girl-cousin, that was the daughter of the dead woman's sister, was there too, and she said, 'When next you see her, you must ask her why she comes.'

The next night the woman appeared again, but the daughter was afraid to speak, and the woman disappeared. She came a third night, and still the daughter was afraid to speak. But the sister's daughter, who was still with her, said, 'God bless you.'

'God bless you, for saying that,' said the woman. And she told them then about her time in the tree and under the bridge. And it was a small enough thing that had brought it about. Then the woman produced a black silk handkerchief, and said, 'I took this from the neck of my husband, when I met him on the road, and he would not stop to help me. And this night, I would have killed him, but now that you have helped me, I will not harm him. But bring you to Kilmacduagh, to the graveyard there, three cross sticks with wool on them, and three glasses full of salt, and have three Masses said for me, and that will give me peace. And when I am at rest, I will come and tell you.'

And the girls did these things, and the woman came to thank them, and said she was now at rest.

Under the Bridge

Under a bridge in Ireland was not a place to look into, especially in the twilight and at night. For it was often there that an unquiet spirit would be confined.

Once in Galway there was a cloth-seller, who went about the countryside selling bolts of cloth. But he was known for giving short measure, never the full yard if he could help it. And when he died, his wife took over his business.

One evening, a traveller was riding up to a bridge, when he found the horse refusing to go on. And he heard a thin, small voice come from under the bridge, and it was the voice of the tailor, who had sold him cloth not long before he died. The voice asked him to give a message to the tailor's wife, and the message was that she should not give short measure, or she would find herself sent to the same place as he himself was in.

A Caring Wife

An islander on Inishmaan was married a long time, but his wife died. After a time, he took a second wife. One evening he was walking home, with his new wife behind him. There was a great wind blowing right into their faces, and he kept his head down because of the wind blowing rain and spray into his eyes. His wife was walking about twenty paces behind him. Something made her look up, and she saw the first wife come and walk close beside her husband. He never saw her, because he had his head down against the wind, but she kept step with him all the way to their house, and then she vanished.

When they were inside the house, the new wife told her husband what she had seen. So great was her fright that she had to take to her bed. Not long after that she died. The husband went on to take a third wife.

The Hand That Would Not Let Go

In the old churchyard at Rathkeale, there was an unquiet spirit, so terrible to look on that anyone who saw its face died soon afterwards. When this happened to some children who had rashly played in the churchyard, a gentleman living nearby determined that something should be done. There was an old woman who lived nearby who was reputed to know about such things, so he went and asked her.

'It needs someone with the courage to go and question it,' said the woman. 'Only that way can it be done away with.'

So the man bravely went to the old churchyard, in the middle of the night, on his horse, and with his sword on his belt, and there he waited. Presently, he saw the shape of the spirit appear in the darkness and move towards him.

'Tell me who you are,' he called.

But as the figure came nearer, its face was so dreadful that his courage failed. He turned the horse's head away, and galloped off as fast as he could go. But after going a long way, he looked down, and he saw the spectre was running with him, and her hand was on the bridle of his horse. Drawing his sword, he took a slash at her, and cut through the arm that was holding the bridle, and at that she vanished.

But when he got home and lit the lamp in his stable, he saw the hand and the cut-off arm still clutching to the bridle. Nothing could get it off. So he left it there, and the horse neighing and shivering, and went into his house, and said his prayers. All night long, there was moaning and crying about the house. But in the morning, when he went to the stable, he found the hand was gone, though there were splashes of blood on the floor. After that, the spirit was never seen in the churchyard again.

The Untended Corpse

There lived a family close to the Galway coast, and the two little girls of it were sent out one day to gather up cow dung. As they sat down by a bush to rest themselves, they heard a strange groaning coming from beneath the ground. Frightened, they ran home as fast as they could. They would not go out again till a man went with them, and they brought the man to the place, and sat down. Before long the same sad groaning began. The man bent his head to the earth and asked what was the matter. A voice from under the earth said, 'Let someone get me out of this and shave me, for I was never shaved after dying.' The man went away, but he came back with soap and all that was needed for shaving, and he found the corpse lying on the grass. So he shaved it, and, with that, wings came and bore it aloft to Heaven.

'You Will Hear Me'

Elliott O'Donnell, the renowned ghost-hunter, was
the six-month-old witness to a strange experience at
the time of his own father's death. His father, a Protestant clergyman, had gone on a tour of the archaeo-
logical sites of Egypt, along with a fellow-clergyman.

On his departure, he said half-jokingly to his wife,
'If anything happens to me while I am away, you will
know of it.'

To which his wife replied, half-seriously, 'Oh, don't
appear in spirit form. You know I have such a horror
of ghosts.'

'Very well,' said the Reverend O'Donnell. 'Should
anything untoward happen, you will not see me. But
you will hear me.'

While he was still away, the household was disturbed and terrified one evening by a horrifying series
of thumps, shouts, and cries. On the following days,
the sound of the minister's footsteps, and his voice,
were frequently heard in the house. Mrs O'Donnell
was full of dire foreboding. Then, sure enough, the
news came through that her husband had been
attacked, robbed and murdered in Egypt.

The Clogher Valley Happenings

At Cavnakirk in the Clogher Valley, in a house that
has since been razed to the ground, lived George
Wilson and his sister. They kept cows and farmed
some acres of mountain ground. They had a younger
brother, but he had been on very bad terms with his

family, especially his sister, and had emigrated to Canada some years before. They had heard nothing from him, and hoped that he would stay away.

One summer evening, George Wilson took his cows down to the byre, left them there for his sister to do the milking, and went in to the kitchen for his supper. From where he sat, he could see through the open door to the byre, where his sister sat milking a cow and singing as she did so. He could hear the hiss of milk going into the pail.

Then he looked away, and as he looked back, he thought he saw a shadowy figure flit across the yard. Then all at once his sister gave a cry, and he got up and rushed out to her. He could hear what sounded like a furious struggle in the byre, and when he went in, he found her half-collapsed against the wall, her face gone black, her eyes staring, as if she were being strangled, while her hands pulled and tugged at her own throat as if trying to dislodge some invisible grip. As her brother came in, the strangling force suddenly abated, and he carried her back to the house.

When she was able to talk, she described what she had seen. Her other brother, who had gone to Canada, appeared round the side of the house. She thought he had returned, but the figure turned dim and shadowy, and abruptly flew at her, seized her by the throat, and started to strangle her. She could feel his grip, and see a shadowy pair of arms and hands, but there was nothing that she herself could get a grip on. Yet she was convinced that if it had not been for George, she would now be lying dead in the byre. When he had come in, she felt the shadowy form loosen its grip, but she had caught a glimpse of an evil, malevolent face, and she recognized it as that of her younger brother.

That night they both went to sleep in the same room, but as soon as night had fallen, a terrible noise began in the kitchen. George Wilson lit a candle and went to investigate, but could see nothing. The noises continued through the night. Next day, the Wilsons told their neighbours what had happened, and two or three volunteered to stay the next night with them. As they sat in the kitchen, all was quiet. But as soon as the kitchen light was put out, and the company moved into the other room, the same crashing, clanging noise broke out in the kitchen. Again, when they went to look, there was nothing to see and no sign of any damage. They returned to the other room and immediately the crashes and thumps resumed, and so it went on all night, and on subsequent nights. George Wilson and his sister were forced to seek the hospitality of their neighbours in order to get a good night's sleep.

At last they enlisted the help of one Richard Robinson, a man who had dealt before with similar situations – he was deeply religious and possessed no fear of ghosts. He stayed in the bedroom with the brother and sister. They lay down on their beds, and he sat with a lighted candle. By and by there was a crash, and a moment later a chair was tipped over. The woman screamed as her bed began to heave up into the air. Robinson slashed beneath it with a sword, and the movement ceased, but another chair went over, and then the bed heaved again. Distracted by a crash from the kitchen, Robinson ran in there to look, but a scream from the sister brought him back. She had seen and felt a dim figure spring on to her bed and reach for her throat.

News came from Canada that the younger Wilson had died there, and when they checked the date, they found his death had occurred on the day of the attack in the byre. Not knowing what was the best thing to do, the two eventually sold their land and emigrated themselves, leaving the baleful spirit of their brother behind.

The Ghost of Captain Dennis

This remarkable story was told by Micheál MacLiammoir, the distinguished actor and co-founder of the Gate Theatre in Dublin. Throughout his life he had a number of encounters with the unexplainable. Born in 1900, and brought up in England, he was old enough by the time of the First World War to have friends who were going off to the Front. In 1916, he said goodbye to Kenneth Dennis, a young Catholic Englishman who had been posted to the Munster Fusiliers and was home on leave. Dennis had a presentiment of his own death and said that he would be killed within three days of returning to France. Young Micheál took this quite casually, and said: 'Do you promise, Kenneth, that you will come back and tell me?'

'Yes, Micheál,' said Dennis, seriously, 'if God allows it, I will come back and tell you.'

He was indeed reported killed within three days, and his friend was grief-stricken for a time, but no ghost appeared. Twenty years later, MacLiammoir was living in Dublin and running the Gate Theatre with his partner Hilton Edwards, with whom he shared an apartment. They had just employed a new man-servant, a Sligo man, who had served in the British Army, and had excellent references. On his first morn-ing, the new man was due to bring MacLiammoir a cup of tea to awaken him at nine o'clock. Just before that, the actor-manager woke up, and heard a step on the stairs. The man's punctual, anyway, he said to himself.

When the door opened he saw a man enter, with a tray, but dressed in the uniform of a British army officer. Such a sight was scarcely to be expected in independent Dublin in 1936. But MacLiammoir realized, with a start, that the young, brown-haired, uniformed visitor was his old friend, Kenneth Dennis. 'Kenneth! Kenneth Dennis – is it you, Kenneth?' he said. The figure nodded, his mouth moving as though he were speaking, though no words could be heard. Then he moved to the curtains and opened them to let the grey morning light stream in. Even as MacLiammoir watched, he saw the figure change, the uniform vanish, and take the shape of an elderly man in the white coat and black trousers of the supe-rior sort of manservant. But the man was looking pale and shaken.

'And what's wrong with you?' asked MacLiammoir.

'Oh, I'm sorry, sir,' he said, 'but didn't I hear you say a name just now – the name, Kenneth Dennis?'

'Yes, he was a very old friend of mine,' replied MacLiammoir. 'I was dreaming, and I – '

But the startled manservant interrupted him to ask if his friend was Captain Dennis of the Munster Fusiliers. When MacLiammoir said that it was, he became even more agitated, and said,

'Oh my God, I knew him – I was Captain Dennis's batman. He died in my arms. In France, in 1916.'

SEABORNE GHOSTS

The Treasure-Bearers of Dunanore

Near the village of Cummer, on Cape Clear, is the remains of an old castle. Called Dunanore, or 'the Golden Fort', it was once the home of the O'Driscolls. In the past, it was linked by a causeway to the mainland, but now it can only be reached by a scramble over tumbled rocks.

The gold in the name 'Golden Fort' has given rise to legends of treasure. It is possible that gold was dug in the country inland. However, it is probably more likely that the castle was a pirates' haven where the gold and other treasure looted from ships out at sea was taken for safekeeping.

One of the stories of Dunanore tells how at night a ghostly ship come in to moor in the bay. Soundlessly, boats are slung from her side and the rowers pull their way from ship to castle, the boats laden with treasure. From the shore the treasure is taken up to the old gateway and the treasure-bearers disappear inside the castle ruins.

Yet it is a ship of dead men, their faces corpse-pale, their clothes slashed by sword-cuts, their bodies showing great wounds. Some of them have their throats cut. Yet still they shoulder their bags, and drag their chests over the rocks, while the bats flit about the gaunt ruin of the broken tower and the shattered walls.

The Ghost Ship

Lady Gregory records the story of an Aran man, Pat O'Hagan:

'One night I was going down to the curragh, and it was a night in harvest, and the stars shining, and I saw a ship fully rigged going towards the coast of Clare, where no ship could go. And when I looked again, she was gone.

'And one morning early, I and other men that were with me, saw a ship coming to the island, and we thought she wanted a pilot, and put out in the curragh. But when we got to where she was, there was no sign of her, but the water was covered with black gulls, and I never saw a black gull before, thousands and crowds of them, and not a white bird among them.

'And one of the boys that was with me took a tarpin and threw it at one of the gulls and hit it on the head, and when he did, the curragh went down to the row-locks in the water – up to that – and it's nothing but a miracle she ever came up again, but we got back to land. I never went to a ship again, for the people said it was on account of me serving in the Preventive Service that it happened, and that if I'd hit at one of the gulls myself, there would have been a bad chance for us. But those were no right gulls, and the ship was no living ship.'

The Lough Derg Boat

Lough Derg, 'the red lough', largest of the Shannon lakes, has its tradition of a ghostly boat, always travelling northwards over its waters. The vessel is a galley, as used by the old Celtic chiefs to travel the waterways of their domains, and those who have seen it claim to have heard the sound of the oars dipping in the water, and also the sounds of voices and low music from within the vessel. Sometimes on dark or misty nights, only the sounds of the passing ship are heard. Yet eyewitnesses have never seen any figure on the deck. Whose ship it was, and what the errand is that she still tries to fulfil, is no longer known.

The Captain

On the coast of Donegal, the islands of Inishinny, Gola and Inismaan form an excellent natural harbour and anchorage, known as Gola Roads. In the late nineteenth century, a small coasting vessel put into the Roads to take refuge from a storm. With their provisions run down, the captain and the two-man crew had to row ashore to the hamlet of Bunbeg to buy food.

They were known to the islanders, who pressed them to stay, because, even within the anchorage, the waves were whipped up by the wind, and breaking on the bar that protected the island. But the captain was anxious to get back to his ship, straining at her anchor cable out in the Roads. They set off in their boat, but never reached the ship.

Next morning the boat was found upside-down on the shore, and the captain's body not far away. The two other men were never found. A message was sent to the ship's owners, and the captain's wife came from

Derry to make arrangements for her husband's funeral.

The island was only inhabited in summer, by a small number of people who put cattle and horses out for summer grazing, gathered driftwood, and fished. Soon after the disaster, they were all gathered in one of the little houses, talking by the fire, when they heard steps coming up to the door. Everyone living on the island was in the room, so they gazed with expectation at who it might be. It was a big man in a peaked cap, wearing nautical clothes – to their surprise and horror, they recognized the very sea-captain whose body had so recently been taken away for burial. At last a woman cried out, in Gaelic, 'Oh, God! Patrick, it's the Captain!' A young man was brave enough to say, 'Come in,' to the figure. But the Captain seemed to move back from the doorway; and in a moment had disappeared. Everybody rushed out, but there was no sign of any other person, nor any footsteps in the sand outside.

SHAPE-SHIFTERS

The Hare and the Butter

Shape-shifting, or the ability of a person to transform him- or herself into an animal, has a long tradition in Irish lore. In the old tradition, the animal is often a deer or a boar, but can also be a bird or even a fly, as in the stories of *The Children of Lir* and of *Etain and Midir*. In more recent encounters, especially if a witch is involved, the animal is often a hare.

A Connemara man, Stephen O'Donnell, recounted to a neighbour (who told Lady Gregory) how he had once shot a hare. The hare promptly turned into a woman, a neighbour of his own. He had a grudge against her, for she had taken his butter (that is to say, charmed his butter production away to add to her own) for two years. But she begged for her life, and he spared her. After that his butter yield doubled.

In a similar account, a man recorded how his uncle was out with his dog when it sprang a hare. The hare ran, and the dog gave chase. The hare made straight for a house, the dog gaining on it, and it gave a great leap over the half-door, whose top section was open. When man and dog came up to the house and looked over the door, there was no hare in the room, only an old woman, nursing a bleeding leg.

The Eel-Woman

Another of Lady Gregory's informants knew of a

woman at Glenlough who could change herself into an eel. This art she had learned in the improbable surroundings of the Galway Workhouse Hospital, where another woman had offered to teach her. It was not an easy transformation, and every time she did it, she would be in bed for a fortnight afterwards. Hearing of this ability, Sir Martin O'Neill got her into a room and made her do it for him. When she did, he became scared, and tried to get away, but the eel went between him and the door, and showed its teeth, and he had to remain there until she changed back.

The Wizard-Earl of Desmond

Lough Gur in County Limerick is in the centre of a region of great historical interest, inhabited from the far-distant past. But the lough itself has a strange legend. Every seven years, the ghost of the last Earl of Desmond is said to rise from the waters and ride across their surface on his great black horse. The horse is shod with silver hooves, and the curse on the Earl is said to be that he must ride these waters once every seven years until the silver on the horse's hooves has been entirely worn away.

The Earl was a practitioner of magic and well-versed in the black arts. Married to a beautiful young wife, he hid these activities from her, but eventually she wanted to know what he did by himself up in his great tower room that overlooked the waters of the lough. For a long time he refused to tell her, but at last, moved by pride in displaying his accomplishments, he agreed to show her what he could do. But he warned her that while she watched on no account must she utter a sound. Promising to obey, his wife followed him up to the chamber. There, as she watched, he transformed himself. First he appeared as a great, gross bird like a vulture. Despite the claws, the carrion smells, and the huge, sharp beak, his wife kept her promise. Then he took the shape of a hideously deformed old woman. The hag approached the countess until they were eye-to-eye, then suddenly disappeared and was replaced by a vast snake that coiled and hissed on the chamber floor. Still the countess kept silent. Finally, her husband resumed his own form, but with a grotesque difference – as if he were made of some stretchable stuff, his body elongated itself until he was immensely long and thin, with his head regarding her from one end of the room and his feet far away at the other. The countess could stand it no longer and gave way to a scream. All went dark, and she fell into a swoon. By and by, when she came to, there was no sign of her husband, but the window shutters stood open. And it was believed that he had sprung, or been thrown, by some supernatural force, into the lough.

(See Appendix, page 188, for another version of this story, ascribed to Garrett Oge Fitzgerald, at Kilkea Castle, Kildare.)

STRANGE HAPPENINGS

The Burnt Stick

Although she was something of a sceptic herself, Lady Augusta Gregory recounted one strange experience of her own. She had gone to Mayo to see the now-ruined house where the poet Raftery had been born. Nearby lived an old woman who was said to be able to see the other world, and Lady Gregory's friend pressed the old woman to talk about 'Those'. But she would not, and instead spoke of America, where she had once lived. But at last she began to talk about what she had seen:

'All I ever saw of them myself was one night when I was going home, and they were behind in the field watching me. I couldn't see them but I saw the lights they carried, two lights on the top of a sort of dark oak pole. So I watched them and they watched me, and when we were tired watching one another the lights all went into one blaze, and then they went away and it went out.'

She also told one or two of the traditional stories, of the man who had a hump put on him, and the woman 'taken', and rescued by her husband, who she had directed to seize the horse she was riding with his left hand.

Then she gave a cry and took up her walking stick from the hearth, burned through, and in two pieces, though the fire had seemed to be but a mouldering heap of ashes. We were very sorry, but she said 'Don't be sorry. It was well it was into it the harm went.'

Lady Gregory recalls, 'I passed the house two or three hours afterwards; shutters and doors were closed, and I felt that she was fretting for the stick that had been to "America and back with me, and had walked every part of the world", and through the loss of which, it may be, she had 'paid the penalty'.

Completing the Round

Dr Aaron Westall was a medical practitioner in County Antrim, who flourished in the late-nineteenth century. An able doctor, he was a popular figure in his locality, with a large number of patients in the countryside. Dr Westall, like many other medical men, liked the good life, with plenty of food and drink. Despite the resultant stoutness, he was also a keen sportsman, with a particular enthusiasm for golf, a sport to which the sandy links of the coast are ideally suited.

One afternoon, he was enjoying a round of golf with two friends (the place is sometimes identified as Portrush); it was a competitive game, and they were playing with a half-sovereign stake on each hole. Westall was having an excellent game and by the thirteenth hole was £8 richer by having won eight holes. But then a lad came running on to the course, calling for the doctor. A patient of his, who lived a mile away, on the Bushmills road, had been taken seriously ill. At first the doctor was reluctant, but then professional ethics prevailed, and he agreed to come immediately.

'But,' he said to his fellow-players, 'I'll be back. I haven't had all my money's worth out of you yet.'

They agreed to wait for him, and he departed at full speed in his gig.

But the doctor never returned. Having treated his patient, he set off again for the golf links, as fast as he could make his horse gallop. But, almost in sight of his destination, and swerving to avoid some hens in the road, he drove into the ditch. The gig overturned, he was thrown out, and killed instantly. The match was never completed.

But when his friends, McGruer and Watson, next went to play golf together, they had a strange experience at the fourteenth hole. Both had played their first shots, and were walking on, when they heard a voice behind them call, 'Fore!' and the unmistakable thwack of an iron striking the ball. Stumbling aside in haste, they looked back, and were amazed to see nobody on the green. But both were utterly convinced that the voice they had heard was that of their recently dead fellow-player, Dr Westall. With some trepidation, they continued their game, but the doctor did not disturb them again.

The Mark of the Five Fingers

This story was told in 1937 by Séamas Ó Cealla of Killeen, County Galway:

'Thomas Harte's uncle was coming home late from his cuaird this night and it was a bright night and the moon was high in the sky. Outside his house was a green flag, and the flag is there to this day. When he was coming in near his home didn't he see the woman on the green flag. He thought it was some neighbouring woman that was there and that it was how she was trying to knock a start out of him. Over he goes and claps his hand on her shoulder. The very minute he did – God bless and save us all and may everyone be well where it is told – she raised her hand and caught him by the crown of the head and lifted him clear up off the road. And she hit him down against the ground again but she did not kill him. He got a terrible fright. And may God bless and save us all, when he got up in the morning the print of her five fingers was on the top of his head and his hair had turned as white as the snow from the dent of his fright.'

The Unsupported Coffin

One of those who wrote to the Reverend John Seymour to share a ghostly experience was a gentleman from County Wexford:

'One night in the month of March 1898 I was driving home with two companions from the house of a relative. We were talking about things in general as our horse trotted leisurely along the lonely midnight road. Things eerie were far from our thoughts. The night was fairly dark, and we had no lamps.

When about halfway on our journey, we saw an object coming slowly towards us. Owing to the imperfect light, we did not notice it until it was within ten yards of our horse's head. It was travelling fair in the middle of the road, and our horse swerved slightly of his own accord before I could pull the rein, and the object also swerved a little to the opposite side. But for this, there would apparently have been a collision.

'No sooner had we passed than we three stared interrogatively at one another. After a moment or two, I exclaimed, "What in Heaven's name was that? Or did you fellows see anything?"

'From their replies they had both seen it as distinctly as I had; and their descriptions tallied in the main with mine.

'After a good deal of discussion we agreed that the object that we had met so unexpectedly was more like a coffin than anything else; and from its slow, swaying motion it appeared to be carried along by invisible bearers. Its height from the ground – some two or three feet – as it moved towards us and past us confirmed this view.

'We saw nothing whatever but the moving coffin – if it was a coffin – and we heard absolutely nothing. There were no bearers, and there was no procession of mourners.

'I may mention that in this county (Wexford) the coffins of the poor are frequently borne to the cemetery by the aid of sheets passed under the coffin and brought through the handles at the sides. Biers on which corpses are borne shoulder-high are not much used.

'I may add that none of us experienced any creepy or uncanny feeling on the occasion, and we were not in the least afraid, even after the passing of the 'ghost'.

We were puzzled and curious, and intensely interested – that was all.'

A Portent for Lord Castlereagh

Robert Stewart, Viscount Castlereagh, was the son of the Marquis of Londonderry. Educated at Armagh and, briefly, Cambridge, he entered politics and became Chief Secretary for Ireland, then later Minister of War in the Westminster Government. In 1822, he committed suicide. As a politician, he had made himself greatly disliked and it was said there was a 'shout of exultation' as his funeral procession made its way to Westminster Abbey.

This story is taken from John H. Ingram's *The Haunted Homes and Family Legends of Great Britain*, published in the 1880s; Ingram himself got it from an earlier compilation, the *Ghost Stories* of Mrs Crowe, published earlier in the nineteenth century. The story is said to originate with Castlereagh's own family, describing an early stage of his career, when he was Captain Robert Stewart, a member of the Dublin Parliament, and was out hunting, somewhere in the north of Ireland.

He was fond of sport, and one day the pursuit of game carried him so far that he lost his way. The weather, too, had become very rough, and in this strait he presented himself at the door of a gentleman's house, and, sending in his card, requested shelter for the night. The hospitality of the Irish country gentry is proverbial. The master of the house received him warmly and said he feared he could not make him as comfortable as he would have wished, his house being full of visitors already. Added to which, some strangers, driven by the inclemency of the night, had sought shelter before him; but that to such accommodation as he could give he was heartily welcome Whereupon the master of the house called his butler, and, committing his guest to his good offices, told the butler he must put Captain Stewart up somewhere, and do the best he could for him. There was no lady, the gentleman being a widower.

Captain Stewart found the house crammed. And a very good party it was. His host invited him to stay, and promised him good shooting if he would prolong his visit a few days. The Captain thought himself extremely fortunate to have fallen into such pleasant quarters.

At length, after an agreeable evening, they all retired to bed, and the butler conducted him to a large room almost divested of furniture, but with a blazing peat fire in the grate, and a shake-down bed on the floor, which was composed of cloaks and other heterogeneous materials. Nevertheless, to the tired limbs of Captain Stewart, who had had a hard day's shooting, it looked very inviting. However, before he lay down, he thought it advisable to take off some of the fire, which was blazing up the chimney in what he thought was an alarming manner. Having done this, he stretched himself upon the couch, and soon fell asleep.

He believed he had slept about a couple of hours when he awoke suddenly, and was startled by such a vivid light in the room that he thought it was on fire;

but on turning to look at the grate saw that the fire was out, though it was from the chimney that the light proceeded.

He sat up in bed, trying to discover what it was, when he perceived, gradually disclosing itself, the form of a beautiful naked boy, surrounded by a dazzling radiance. The boy looked at him earnestly, and then the vision faded, and all was dark.

Captain Stewart, so far from supposing what he had seen to be of a spiritual nature, had no doubt that the host, or the visitors, had been amusing themselves at his expense, and trying to frighten him. Accordingly, he felt indignant at the liberty; and on the following morning, when he appeared at breakfast, he took care to evince his displeasure by the reserve of his demeanour, and by announcing his intention to depart immediately. The host expostulated, reminding him of his promise to stay and shoot. Captain Stewart coldly excused himself, and at length, the gentleman, seeing something was wrong, took him aside and pressed for an explanation; whereupon Captain Stewart, without entering into any particulars, said he had been made the victim of a sort of practical joking that he thought quite unwarrantable with a stranger. The gentleman considered this not impossible amongst a parcel of thoughtless young men, and appealed to them to make an apology; but one and all, on their honour, denied the impeachment.

Suddenly a thought seemed to strike him: he clapped his hand to his forehead, uttered an exclamation, and rang the bell.

'Hamilton,' said he to the butler, 'where did Captain Stewart sleep last night?'

'Well, sir,' replied the man, in an apologetic tone, 'you know every place was full – the gentlemen were lying on the floor three or four in a room – so I gave him *the boy's room*; but I lit a blazing fire to keep *him* from coming out.'

'You were very wrong,' said the host. 'You know I have positively forbidden you to put anyone there, and have taken the furniture out of the room to ensure it's not being occupied.'

Then retiring with Captain Stewart, he informed him very gravely of the nature of the phenomenon he had seen; and at length, being pressed for further information, he confessed that there existed a tradition in his family that whoever the 'radiant boy' appeared to would rise to the summit of power, and when he reached the climax, would die a violent death.

'And I must say,' he added, 'the records that I have kept of his appearance go to confirm this persuasion.'

In the years after this experience, Stewart's career indeed took him to the summit of political life – almost – for he never became prime minister. Nevertheless, it was while still in office that, believing himself to be blackmailed for his homosexuality, he committed suicide at his house in England.

The vision of the 'radiant boy' seems to have been an unusual one in Ireland, though it has been recorded from places in England and Germany. It is not always seen as a portent. Sometimes it is related to the murder of a child in the house. Clearly it is a phenomenon of great power.

The Thing in the Lodgings

Elliott O'Donnell, who died in 1965 aged almost ninety, was, as we have seen, a lifelong student of the paranormal. As a young college student in Dublin, he had an alarming experience in a lodging house close to the Waterloo Road. After spending the evening with student friends who lived in the same house, he had gone to bed.

As usual, he locked his room door, then put out the light and got into bed. The room had thick curtains, but rays of moonlight filtered through the gap, and in the shafts of light, O'Donnell saw something move. He looked more intently at the place, and was horrified to see what he later called 'the shape of something dark and sinister' rise up from the floor, without a sound, and swiftly approach his bed. Lying down, a person always feels more helpless in any sort of predicament, and O'Donnell felt the familiar sense of powerlessness as the presence loomed up over him.

He could not move a muscle, or make a sound, despite his feeling of panic. As he lay there, he felt the 'thing' whose shape was indistinct in the darkness, suddenly leap at him. Strong bony fingers gripped him around the throat and pressed him back against the mattress. Gasping and choking, he tried to struggle free but the strength of the strangling fingers was too great. O'Donnell felt a buzzing in his ears and felt certain his death was upon him. Then he lost consciousness.

When he came to, some time later, there was no sign of his assailant. He struck a light and examined the room carefully. The door was still locked, the window bolted on the inside, but the room appeared to be empty of all but the usual furnishings. So little time had passed that he could still hear his friends talking elsewhere in the house. O'Donnell was already no stranger to ghostly manifestations, or he might have fled the room there and then. Instead, not without trepidation, he tried to settle back to sleep. Eventually he did fall asleep, and when he woke, it was with the same sensation as before – that something horribly sinister was right by his bedside. The sky was already beginning to turn grey outside. He pulled the bedclothes over his head and lay curled up there until he heard the landlady knock on his door.

He asked the landlady to give him another room, which she did without demur, and he moved his things out of the haunted room that day. But it was only when he came to leave her house for good that the landlady admitted that other people had had frightening experiences in his first bedroom. At an earlier time, the house had been a sort of private asylum for the care of the insane. In that room, although she did not know the details, someone had been violently killed.

This was the experience which, O'Donnell said, turned him into a ghost hunter. For all his terror, he was also intrigued by what had happened to him, and by what must have happened at one time in that room to preserve in it such a tangible spirit of malevolence and murderous impulse.

The Thing on the Bicycle

In 1910, Thomas Fahey, a neighbour of the Reverend John Seymour, had some alarming moments as he rode his bicycle along the country road from the village of Cappawhite in Tipperary. He was extremely familiar with every detail of the route, having travelled it hundreds of times before. About a third of a mile before Ironmills Bridge there was a cottage in a garden, with a boreen leading up on the left side into the fields. Just by the end of this boreen, the road drops steeply for a hundred yards, to a point where another boreen runs up on the left; then it continues on a more gentle downhill grade towards the bridge. It was an autumn evening, becoming dark but bright enough for him to see his way without a lamp. Just as he came to the cottage and its garden, and was preparing to freewheel down the hill, something emerged abruptly from the boreen. How it moved he could not tell – but it came to rest on the handlebars of his bicycle. He described it as resembling a large round bundle, that seemed to be black in colour. It was like no animal, and remained where it was without sound, or movement, or smell of any kind. It was large enough for him to have to sit well back on the saddle to prevent his face from coming in contact with it; and he could just see over the top of it.

The arrival of the thing, whatever it was, made no

impact, but the shock of its sudden appearance made the rider wobble, though he was able to preserve his balance. He might have jumped from his bicycle, but he decided that the best thing for him to do was to keep on moving, and so he did. But instead of coasting down the hill, he found his machine had grown so difficult to move that it was only by pushing hard on the pedals that he was able to keep it moving at all. In this way, he laboured down to the bottom of the steep hill, where at the second boreen, the thing left him as suddenly as it had come, and vanished up the pathway. Immediately the drag on the bicycle was removed, and it freewheeled easily on down towards the bridge, bearing its shaken and baffled rider.

The Phantom of York Road Station

'I was sitting in one of the carriages in the shed and there was nobody about. Suddenly one of the rings on a fire extinguisher on the platform came flying down the coach. It landed at my feet and when I picked it up, it felt warm.'

This is how Sally Davidson, a carriage cleaner, described her experience at the recently rebuilt York Road Station in Belfast. At the same place, a guard in the train heard the sound of footsteps walking on the stone ballast on the other side from the platform, but when he looked out, there was no one to be seen. Late at night, someone was seen sitting in the canteen, which had been locked from the outside. When staff opened the door, the 'someone' had disappeared.

Who or what is the phantom of York Road? There has been a station and carriage yard here for a long time; it was once the terminus of the Larne line before central Belfast's new railway system was built. But it seems that it is only since the new tracks and buildings have been there, that the strange happenings have been noted.

Who knows what the rebuilding disturbed – this area of Belfast was heavily bombed during the war, with much damage and loss of life. Or is it some long-dead railway servant, killed by accident or enemy action, who still walks the tracks and drifts about the buildings?

The Comb

This account is by Séamas O Cealla, told in Patricia Lysaght's *The Banshee*:

'A young man called Regan, from Killeen in Galway, was coming home from the bog, where he had been digging out a stump of a tree, 'bog deal' as it was known, which people used to split into long spills. Dipped in tallow, these were then used as lights, as a substitute for lamps or candles. As he came on his way home, in the gathering dusk, he reached a stream and there he heard the familiar banging sound (in those days long before detergents) of a woman washing clothes and using her beetle, or wooden mallet, to beat the garments. Then he saw the figure of a woman, the beetle in one hand and a fine comb in the other. Perhaps he knew it was the bean *sí*, but if he did, it made no difference. Quickly he stepped up behind her, and in a spirit of roguery, snatched the comb from her hand. Then he leapt across the stream and made for home.

The supernatural being raised a fearful scream, and in a moment she was after him in pursuit. He was a fast runner, and that was lucky for him. She threw her beetle and it whistled past his ear. He kept on running, and when she came up to it she threw it again, and this time he felt its wind part his hair. Regan ran on, and just he reached his house, the woman caught up the beetle and threw it a third time, and it crashed against the gable, shaking the house from top to bottom. He rushed inside, bolted the door and secured the wooden door-bar right across it. Outside, the woman gave an unearthly, bloodcurdling wail and within the wail, they could hear words in Irish, telling them to return the comb or she would tear the house down.

Regan found a spade, and, placing the comb on the iron blade, slid the spade beneath the door. When he pulled it back in again it was oddly light – not only the comb but all the iron of the spade was gone. But the fairy woman had departed, and all was quiet again. Next morning, when he went out to look at the house, he saw that the gable end was split from thatch to ground, as a result of the stroke from her beetle.

Experiences of an Engineer's Wife

Ireland was once networked by rural railways, providing a transport service that was revolutionary to those who had only known the donkey and cart. One of these was the Collooney and Claremorris line, now long disappeared. But while it was being built, the Resident Engineer rented a cottage close to Collooney, and he and his wife lived there, so that he could be in close touch with the works. The engineer had regular meetings with the contractors and foremen, and these often turned into social events and continued into the evening. His wife did not wait up for him, but went to bed early, leaving the door on the latch so that he could let himself in.

On one such evening, she went to bed and fell asleep, and after a time was awakened by hearing footsteps in the sitting room next to the bedroom, which then entered the bedroom itself. Next she felt a hand rest on her shoulder, and sat up in the dark, thinking it was her husband returned.

'What is the matter?' she said. But there was no answer. Then she heard the footsteps going back across the sitting room, and a voice which she did not recognize called, 'Goodnight! Goodnight!' Thinking it to be some joke of her husband's, she went back to sleep.

Some time after that, she was again awakened by a tapping at the window – there was no upper floor – and heard her husband's voice, asking to be let in. Feeling angry at being wakened by him for the second time, she got up and let him into the house. The door was indeed no longer on the latch.

'What on earth possessed you to come in, touch me, and then go out again?' she demanded. But her husband had been at the hotel with his colleagues all the time. He put her experience down to a nightmare, and asked jokingly what she had had for supper on the previous evening.

But after that, both he and she noticed many strange things. Someone would knock at the bedroom door, but when it was opened, there was no one there. There were shoutings, and noises as if a fire were being violently poked. The lady one day recounted some of these experiences to a friend, a doctor who lived some way from the cottage. He heard her without surprise, then he shook his head and said:

'I don't wonder! I had a great friend, a cultured man, who was an inspector of national schools. He used to come round here periodically and put up at the cottage; and when he did he always used to send over for me to come and dine, and spend a pleasant evening with him.

'About two years ago, he came as usual, writing to me beforehand to say what day to expect him. I went accordingly in anticipation of the pleasure his visit always gave me. But I found him silent and morose, not at all like his usual pleasant self. He ate nothing, nor did he drink anything, and after the meal was over we sat in silence by the fireside, having a smoke, which he did not seem to enjoy either.

'At length, I became weary of doing and saying nothing, so rising and pushing back my chair, I said, "My dear fellow, what is wrong with you? I never saw you in such a mood before. You won't eat, drink, or talk! Why," I added in jest, "you seem like a man who is contemplating suicide! I am going home, and

I hope that the next time we meet you will be better company."

'So saying I bade him adieu, mounted my horse, and rode off. I had barely reached home when a messenger came hotfoot after me to say my poor friend had put an end to himself, and would I see if I could do anything for him. I returned as quickly as I could, and, on arriving at the cottage, found that he had cut his throat, and was beyond the reach of human aid.'

Undaunted by the doctor's tale, the lady and her husband stayed on in the cottage, with its knocks and noises, until his job was finished.

The Old Fisherman

As a young man, still a student, Arthur Frewen, the playwright and schoolmaster, was walking on the Waterford coast near Helvick Head. The day turned misty and dark, and he began to look ahead anxiously for the lights of a village where he might find a bed for the night. As he came to the expected village and walked among the houses, he found the place oddly deserted and dark.

The first light he saw came from the little pier, and walking along it, he found himself looking down on the deck of a fishing boat. The hatchway was open and as he stood there, the grizzled face of an elderly seaman appeared in it. Frewen asked if he could have the use of a bunk for the night, and the man gruffly agreed. He showed the young man through to the fo'c'sle where a bunk was built into each side. Frewen took off a red scarf of his sister's that he was wearing, and hung it on the door between the fo'c'sle and the cabin, where the old man sat mending a net. Presently, the old man called him through, and gave him a meal of potato soup.

Frewen then went to lie down in his bunk, but almost as soon as he lay down, instead of dropping off to sleep, a growing feeling possessed him that something was wrong, that something terrible was going to happen. Eventually his terror grew to such a pitch that he got up, and slid the bolt in the door to bar it. Immediately after that he felt the door being tried. It rattled, and shook.

Then there was a hard pounding on it and a furious voice cried, 'Open up!' Frewen was certainly not going to do that. As the battering on the door increased, he heaved himself up on the bunk, smashed through the thick glass of the little window fitted in the deck, hoisted himself out, sprang from the boat to the pier, and ran for his life.

He stayed out the rest of the night, but when morning came, he walked into the village and found it a normal little hamlet, with people going about their morning business. Someone commented on his scratched and haggard appearance, and he blurted out the story of his night's experience.

'It was that boat, tied up just there,' he said.

The man to whom he was speaking looked at him strangely, then walked with him to the pier. There was no fishing boat. Canted against the side of the pier was the derelict remnant of a boat, its timbers warped and slimy, with great cracks in the side and the deck, at first sight nothing like the trim vessel with its bunks and stove. But yet, as he looked at it incredulously, he saw it was the same sort of boat, with an open hatchway down to a central cabin, and a square hole in the foredeck, where the skylight window of the fo'c'sle would have been, its glass long since vanished.

'This boat has been mouldering here for nearly fifty years,' said the local. 'There is a bad story about it.'

He explained that, fifty years before, a young student on a walking holiday had been murdered on board this boat. The fisherman had been arrested, convicted of the crime, and hanged at Dungarvan. Ever since then the vessel had lain there.

Emboldened by the daylight and the presence of the interested villagers, young Frewen scrambled down into the decayed vessel. There was nothing in its hull but sand and seaweed. But when he pushed open, with great difficulty, the door between cabin and fo'c'sle, there, on a nail in the door, was hanging his red scarf.

The Midnight Cavalry

Mr William Mackey of Strabane related a strange late-night experience he had whilst out shooting in the winter of 1852:

'It was a bitterly cold night towards the end of November or the beginning of December; the silvery moon had sunk in the west shortly before midnight; the sport had been all that could be desired, when I began to realize that the blood was frozen in my veins, and I was on the point of starting for home, when my attention was drawn to the barking of a dog close by, which was followed in a few seconds by the loud report of a musket, the echo of which had scarcely died away in the silent night when several musket-shots went off in quick succession; this seemed to be the signal for a regular fusillade of musketry, and it was quite evident from the nature of the firing that there was attack and defence.

'For the life of me I could not understand what it all meant. Not being superstitious, I did not for a moment imagine it was supernatural, notwithstanding that my courageous dog was crouching in abject terror between my legs; beads of perspiration began to trickle down my forehead, when suddenly there arose a flame as if a house were on fire, but I knew from the position of the blaze (which was only a few hundred yards from where I stood) that there was no house there, or any combustible that would burn, and what perplexed me most was to see pieces of burning thatch and timber sparks fall hissing into the water at my feet.

'When the fire seemed at its height the firing appeared to weaken, and when the clear sign of a bugle floated out on the midnight air, it suddenly ceased, and I could hear distinctly the sound of cavalry coming at a canter, their accoutrements jingling quite plainly on the frosty air; in a very short time they arrived at the scene of the fight. I thought it an eternity until they took their departure, which they did at the walk.

'It is needless to say that, although the scene of this tumult was on my nearest way home, I did not venture that way, as, although there are many people who would say that I never knew what fear was, I must confess on this occasion I was thoroughly frightened.

'At breakfast, I good a good sound rating from my father for staying out so late. My excuse was that I fell asleep and had a horrible dream, which I related. When I finished, I was told that I had been dreaming with my eyes open – that I was not the first person who had witnessed this strange sight. He then told me the following narrative:

'"It was towards the end of the seventeenth century that a widow named Sally Mackey and her three sons lived on the outskirts of the little settlement of the Mackeys. A warrant was issued by the Government against the three sons for high treason, the warrant being delivered for execution to the officer of the infantry regiment stationed at Lifford. A company of troops set off from Lifford for the purpose of effecting the arrest at eleven that night.

'"The cottage home of the Mackeys was approached by a bridlepath, leading from the main road to Derry, which only permitted the military to arrive in single file; they arrived there at midnight, and the first intimation the inmates had of danger was the barking, and then the shooting, of their collie dog. Possessing as they did several stand of arms, they opened fire on the soldiers as they came in view and killed and wounded several. It was the mother, Sally Mackey, who did the shooting, the sons loading the

muskets. Whether the cottage went on fire by accident or design was never known; it was only when
the firing from the cottage ceased and the door was
forced open that the officer in command rushed in
and brought out the prostrate form of the lady, who
was severely wounded and burned. All the sons perished, but the soldiers suffered severely, a good many
being killed and wounded.

"'The firing was heard by the sentries at Lifford,
and a troop of cavalry was despatched to the scene of
conflict, but only arrived in time to see the heroine
dragged from the burning cottage. She had not, however, been fatally wounded, and lived for many years
afterwards with a kinsman. My father remembered
conversing with old men, when he was a boy, who
remembered her well. She seemed to take a delight
in narrating incidents of the fight to those who came
to visit her, and would always finish up by making
them feel the pellets between the skin and her ribs.'"

The Haunted Mantelpiece

A marble mantelpiece, originally from Dunsandle
House in County Galway, was bought by a sculptor
in Dublin, Christy O'Neill. He was busy in his work-
shop, late one evening, when he happened to glance
towards the mantelpiece, which had been placed inside. To his surprise, he saw the shadowy figure of a
tall man standing beside it. When he moved towards
it, the figure vanished. But immediately afterwards,
pieces of marble rose up apparently of their own accord and moved about the studio, and both the sculp-

tor and his family heard strains of music. O'Neill made some inquiries at Dunsandle and was told that the tall ghost had indeed been seen in the castle, but not since the fireplace had been sold.

This tale came to the attention of the American ghost-hunter, Hans Holzer, during a visit to Ireland. Holzer received a further account from Roger Kilbride, who in 1940 had been part of a detachment of soldiers billetted in Dunsandle House. He was a cook-sergeant and with his team was bedded down in the dining room, when about fifteen minutes after midnight they heard the sound of a violin playing. They attributed it to another member of the troop, one Carmody, who had a violin on which he played Irish airs. But this, they agreed, was not Irish but 'high class classical stuff'. And next morning they found that Carmody had pawned his fiddle; and that there had definitely been no radio playing. The mystery of the music was not resolved, and they did not hear it again.

But, in 1957, Roger Kilbride read a story in a newspaper, *The Sunday Review*, about a haunted fireplace from Dunsandle House. When it was vacated by the army in 1945, the owners of Dunsandle House moved back in, and sold various items, including the fireplace, to a dealer in Dublin, who installed the fireplace in his own sitting room. But when he found that strange violin music emanated from it, he had the fireplace taken out.

Holzer contacted the owners of the castle, in the course of 1965, and was informed that Dunsandle was now in a ruinous state. The owners had transferred the mantelpiece to their new home at Clonagh Castle, in County Offaly, but no music came from it. Where the haunted mantelpiece may now be, and what caused the violin music, is apparently not known.

St Patrick's Bell

In legend, St Patrick is reputed to have rid Ireland of snakes, toads and other undesirable creatures by ringing his bell at the edge of a cliff and then throwing it over. The creatures followed it over the brink, to fall to their deaths, but the bell was each time returned to the saint by angelic hands.

Some pilgrims making the ascent of Croagh Patrick have heard the sound of a handbell rung from the top as they struggled up. Unlike the snakes, they found the sound encouraging and revivifying, and it helped them to complete the arduous climb to the summit. But there was no one with a bell when they reached the oratory on the mountain-top. This phenomenon has been particularly noticed during the forty days of Lent.

The Strabane Station Ghost

Strabane nowadays is far from a railway line, but until the 1950s it was a railway centre of some importance, where narrow-gauge lines from Glenties, Killybegs and Letterkenny in Donegal met the standard-gauge main line with connections to all the main cities of Ireland. One October night, three men, named as

Madden, Oliphant and Pinkerton, were at work in the engine-shed, preparing an engine for an early departure. Shortly after midnight, they heard a terrific sound of knocking or hammering, which seemed to come from all over the building. This hammering was punctuated by a series of hideous screams and wailings. Opening up the doors, they were confronted by the huge figure of a man, glaring at them. Alerted by the same noises, another railwayman came running up from outside. He had taken the precaution of picking up a heavy spanner used for tightening rail joints, but the weapon made no impression at all on the figure, which remained present for almost two hours. The men, frightened to leave the engine-shed, stayed there until it finally vanished.

The spectre returned the following night, when the same men were again on the night shift. Oliphant approached it, in an effort to find out whether it really was solid or not, but became overwhelmed by fear and collapsed. Again the figure uttered horrendous cries, and various objects, such as tools and pieces of machinery, were tossed about inside the engine-shed.

Although it transpired that a murder had been committed close to that spot, long before the days of railways, the manifestation has never really been explained.

The Publican's Widow

Another pair of engine cleaners were subjected to a shock on a mid-September night in 1918. On duty from seven in the evening to seven in the morning, it was their usual custom to go every night to fill up a can of drinking water from a pump slightly more than a quarter of a mile from the engine-shed. On this particular night, two men went along, leaving the engine shed at about half past twelve. The night was described as soft and fine, and not very dark. Their way to the pump took them past a public house on the lefthand side and a graveyard on the right. Of course, at that time of night everything was closed, shuttered, silent.

Both men felt that the night was unusually quiet and still, but as they came by the cemetery, both felt a heavy blast of chilly wind, and at the same time a mournful wailing sound sprang up. They stopped and looked around, but the wind and the sound died away as abruptly as they had come. Without a word, the two men went on, and in a few yards reached the public house.

This was kept by a widow, whose husband had died only six months before and was buried in the nearby graveyard. There were two doors to the premises, one opening on to the street, the other in a side lane. As they passed, they suddenly heard a vehement knocking at the side door. They looked down the lane, but could see nothing but the empty narrow way. Then there came a terrible cry, described by one as like a dog in awful agony. The two cleaners went on to fill their can, and on the return journey, no doubt made with beating hearts, they heard and felt nothing. They went home after their shift was done, and went to bed; but when they woke up, they learned that the landlady of that same public house had suffered a stroke and died during the very early hours of the morning.

The Phantom Train

At a railway station, on the now-closed and torn-up line from Clones to Armagh, two men were waiting for a train on a summer evening in 1924. It was a quiet wayside station and there was no one waiting but themselves. As they sat on a platform bench, outside the waiting room, they could hear the sound of voices from inside – low, hurried voices, punctuated by terrible moans and groans, which gradually got louder. At last, one of the two got up and put his face against the waiting room window, to see what was going on in there. But he saw that the narrow room, furnished with two benches and a long table, had nobody in it at all.

He resumed his seat, and then he and his companion heard the sound of a train, coming up fast. They got expectantly to their feet, as the puffing and clattering increased, and looked down the line which curved away into a cutting. The noise reached a peak, and they involuntarily jumped back, hearing a horrifying human scream just as the engine seemed to rush past them with a piercing whistle. But no train appeared. The sound dwindled away, with the tracks as empty as they had been before, and both men sank back on to their bench, exchanging scared looks. A few moments later, the signalman came out of his office, ready to pick up the token from the engine-driver. He had heard nothing, but told them that a man had jumped in front of a train at that same station just a year before, and had been brought, critically injured, into the waiting room, and had died there on the long table.

The Ambush Ghosts

Two miles outside Listowel, there is a gate by a cross-roads where three IRA men were lying in wait for a Black and Tan patrol in 1918. The ambush went wrong, and two of them were shot by the British Irregulars. In later years, a Celtic cross was put up at the site.

But long before that, later in the same year that the incident took place, two young men, Patrick Moloney and Moss Barney, were cycling along the road towards Listowel, at about one in the morning on a bright moonlit night. Earlier that evening, they had been to a circus and were riding along in high spirits. When they reached the scene of the shootings, something made them come to a stop. Although both desired to continue, there was some force that was detaining them, as if their machines were being held back by strong unseen hands.

As Patrick Moloney recounted it, he had the sensation that someone was trying to keep them back from some trouble further down the road. The road was level, yet to break away from the force that stayed him was a tremendous physical effort. Sweating and shaky, at last he managed to pull away. A short distance on, as they passed a stretch of wood, the invisible power was released. Both men had felt the same thing.

A Portent at Tullamore

The Marquess of Dufferin and Ava was a great British grandee, a former Viceroy of India. In the autumn of 1890, as a guest at the big country house of Tullamore, not far from Wexford, he was enjoying the restful quietness of the Irish countryside. During his stay, he went up to his room one night, close to midnight. A log fire was burning in the hearth and he decided to read for a time before going to sleep. But when he put the book aside, he felt wakeful and restless. After a time, he dozed off but soon woke up again, though normally he went quickly and soundly to sleep. On this night, however, he found himself twisting and turning and quite unable to settle down; a strange sense of dread seemed to have taken possession of him.

At last he got out of bed. It was almost two o'clock in the morning. Walking across the room to the window, he parted the curtains and looked out. It was a bright night of full moon, without a cloud in the sky. The moon's pale radiance made everything in the garden stand out with great clarity. Lord Dufferin looked out at the calm and motionless scene, hoping that it might have a soothing effect on his restless mind, when he saw someone move down in the garden. The figure of a man came out of the shadow on to the open expanse of lawn. He was carrying something large and long on his back, the weight of which bent him almost double. His slow progress came to a stop when he was just below the ex-Viceroy's window; and there he straightened himself up and looked up towards the window and the man looking down from it.

The moonlight showed a face full of evil and malevolence, so much so that Lord Dufferin took a step backwards from his window; but it remained etched into his memory. When he looked again, the man had resumed his slow progress, carrying the long, weighty object, which, Dufferin suddenly realized with a shudder of shock, was a coffin.

The Marquess was convinced that he had seen no ghost and in any case he did not believe in ghosts. The figure had seemed all too real, and had cast a shadow in the bright moonlight. He went back to bed, and despite or because of the shock, immediately fell fast asleep. When he told his host and fellow-guests about what he had seen, they found it hard to take the story seriously. The house had no history of hauntings or strange happenings. He put the event at the back of his mind, and it did not deter him from further visits to Tullamore. However, the strange sight never repeated itself.

A long time later, the Marquess of Dufferin was on a visit to Paris, where he was due to address a gathering of diplomats. The meeting was in the salon on the fifth floor of a Paris hotel. The hotel manager escorted him to the lift, and as the lift doors opened, Lord Dufferin's eyes fell on the lift attendant. The man's face was the face he had seen long ago at Tullamore, but never forgotten. The same sense of dread returned. Just about to step into the lift, the Marquess turned abruptly back and waved it away. Several other people got in, and, watched by the curious and surprised hotel manager, he waited, hearing it rise floor by floor. Then there was a sudden clanging noise, a scream, and a terrible thudding that resounded through the building floor by floor. The lift cable had snapped just before the fifth floor. The lift fell and its occupants, including the operator, were killed.

Shaken by the experience, Lord Dufferin was even more surprised when it turned out that the operator was not the normal one; he had been engaged on that day, and no one appeared to know who he was or where he had come from.

The Shelbourne Ghost

In August 1965, the American ghost hunter and author, Hans Holzer, stayed in Dublin's Shelbourne Hotel with his wife and the British medium, Sybil Leek. They were looking for evidence of hauntings in and around the city, and were taken by surprise to come across a ghost in the hotel itself. Sybil Leek became aware of it in her little top-floor room. Unable to sleep, she had sat up very late, writing, and was lying awake in bed some time after two o'clock in the morning, when she heard a noise that seemed to be a child crying.

She quietly called, 'What's the matter?'

A little voice answered, 'I'm frightened.'

'Come to me then,' said Miss Leek, whose training and experience had taught her to take such things calmly; and she felt a small figure climb on to her bed, and what she described as the touch of a light woolly material across her right cheek and her outstretched right arm. She fell asleep, and when she awoke in the morning, her arm was numb, as though some weight had been pressing on it all night. The next evening, Sybil Leek was on the lookout, and was able to speak to the ghost, that of a girl of seven, who said her name was Mary Masters.

The following night, Miss Leek, in a trance, was able to hold a conversation with Mary, of which she remembered nothing when she came to again. Hans Holzer noted that the child appeared to be ill, suffering from a cold or bad throat, and was asking for a bigger sister named Sophie. The Shelbourne Hotel is formed from several houses, and acquires a lot of its character from the resulting up-and-down passages. He concluded that it was a child who had died in one of these houses, around 1846 – a date which Sybil Leek had found herself writing down the day before, without knowing why.

THE 'TAKEN'

Fairies or Wild Spirits

The fairies, or wild spirits of the Irish countryside, were notorious for their snatching of human children. Boys especially were at risk. Many old photographs vouch for the fact that in the far west of Ireland, and well into the twentieth century, many boys even of ten or eleven were kept in dresses, to fool the fairies into supposing they were girls. One of W. B. Yeats's most haunting poems is the fairies' call to the mortal child:

'Come away, o human child,
To the waters and the wild,
For the world's more full of weeping than you can understand.'

Mrs Sheridan's Child

Old Mrs Sheridan 'was wrinkled and half-blind, and had gone barefoot through her lifetime', according to Lady Gregory. But she was in contact with the invisible world. Among her stories of children that were taken was one of her own:

'There was a child I had, and he a year and a half old, and he got a quinsy and a choking in the throat and I was holding him in my arms beside the fire, and all in a minute he died. And the men were working down by the river, washing sheep, and they heard the crying of a child from over there in the air, and they said, "That's Sheridan's child." So I knew sure enough that he was *taken*.'

The Ballymacduff Drownings

Another of Mrs Sheridan's stories was both more circumstantial and more gruesome.

'One time when I was living at Ballymacduff there was two little boys drowned in the river there, one was eight years old and the other eleven years. And I was out in the fields, and the people looking in the river for their bodies, and I saw a man coming away from it, and the two boys with him, he holding a hand of each and leading them away. And he saw me stop and look at them, and he said, "Take care, would you bring them from me, she'll never come home to you again." And one of the little chaps broke from his hand and ran to me, and the other cried out to him, "Oh, Pat, would you leave me!" So then he went back and the man led them away. And then I saw another man, very tall he was, and crooked, and watching me like this with his head down and he was leading two dogs the other way, and I knew well where he was going and what he was going to do with them.

'And when I heard the bodies were laid out, I went to the house to have a look at them, and those were never the two boys that were lying there, but the two dogs that were put in their places. I knew this by the sort of stripes on the bodies such as you'd see in the covering of a mattress; and I knew the boys couldn't be in it, after me seeing them led away.'

The 'Taken' Bride

In Galway in the nineteenth century, a man from Duras married a girl from Ardrahan. The wedding was at the bride's home, and at the end of it, the young couple left for the groom's house, she riding behind her uncle on his horse, as it was customary for the bride to be escorted to her new home by her nearest male relative.

As they were passing by the churchyard at Ardrahan, the uncle felt her break out into a fit of shivering so violent that she almost fell off the horse. When he asked her what ailed her, she said that passing the graveyard had caused her to think of her dead mother. He put his hand behind to help support her, but her body felt as limp as a piece of tow.

They arrived eventually at the groom's house, and she lived there for a year, and had a baby. But she died giving birth to the child. Everyone, however, believed that the night she was taken was that of her wedding.

Biddy Purcell

Carrigogunnell Castle, near Limerick, is famously described in Frank McCourt's memoir of his boyhood, *Angela's Ashes*. But long before that, its ruins had a reputation for spookiness.

Biddy Purcell was a bright, cheerful young girl of eighteen or so, who went one Sunday with her sister and other girls to pick rushes from the boggy land between the castle and the River Shannon. Just as they were passing the castle gateway, a small child, or what seemed to be one, came out and gave Biddy a touch between the shoulder blades with a switch of wood. She felt a strange pain pass through her, into her heart, and out again. But the other girls laughed, and on they went to gather rushes.

Biddy was by herself and had gathered a good pile of rushes, when a strange, little old woman came up to her and said,

'Biddy Purcell, give me some of your rushes.'

Something about the old woman made Biddy afraid, but she still said, 'The bog is big enough for everyone; pluck your own.'

The little old woman flew into a rage, and gave the girl a slash across the knees and feet with a little whip she had.

Now, with the pain at her heart, and the pain in her legs and feet, Biddy was in a bad way. She stumbled home crying, and lay sick in her bed for five days. She told her sister that she had seen a vision of fairy men riding out from underneath the castle, and all but one had a girl mounted behind him; that one was waiting for her.

The family sent for a man supposed to have skill in bringing people back, and he made a potion of herbs which he told them to boil. If it turned green, then Biddy might still be saved; if it turned yellow, then she was already too far gone.

The potion turned yellow, and when they gave it to her to drink, she very soon after died. And though she was given a Christian burial, there were those who believed that the company of riders under

Carrigogunnell Castle was now at last complete.

(*See also* 'Cormac and Mary' in the Appendix, page 186.)

APPENDIX – GHOST VERSES

The Ghost of Boho
(A verse tale)

One Hallowe'en the moon shone low
And dimly lit the graves of Boho;
A peasant, destined for exile,
Leave-taking, crossed the temple stile;
But in the graveyard's middle ways
A ghostly spectre met his gaze!
Just by the grave of Seamus Dhu,
It stood erect, full in his view.
Now, startled by this spectral sight,
McFadden trembled with the fright,
And turned around to flee the place –
But now he found the ghost gave chase.
Though hard he runs to reach the stile,
The ghost gains on him all the while:
Alas for Jim, he takes a fall
Headlong he goes o'er the churchyard wall;
The ghost, pursuing in his track,
Went headlong o'er McFadden's back.
With fear the man was nearly dead,
When the ghost stood calmly there and said,
'Ah, sure I only meant it just for fun,
To show you how a ghost could run.

But come, we'll put a stop to tricks
And chat a bit about politics.'
This said, the ghost quite leisurely
Leaned his back against a tree:
'Tell me how the fighting goes,
And are the landlords still your foes?
They were the villains long ago
And terrorized us here in Boho.
And is the law as bad of late
As it was in ninety-eight?
What do you think of Lawyer Dan –
Is he an honest-hearted man?'
'Ah, that he is, indeed,' said Jim,
'I wish we had a score like him.
You find me when my mind is troubled:
My rent this day – ten pound – was doubled,
And this is far too much to pay
For a bit of bog and rocky brae.
No wonder that my spirit's low –
Tomorrow morning I must go
To earn my bread on a foreign shore
And leave old Ireland that I adore.'
'You will not leave,' the ghost replied;
'Rest! There is a turning of the tide;
This very night I'll take a walk
And with your landlord I will talk.
And, if he proves unkind, I'll show
The fellow what a ghost can do.
Come with me, for you know they say
A chat makes short a longsome way.'
To see the fun Jim's heart was bent,

They set their hats and off they went
O'er highroad, byroad, meadow, stile,
They travelled on for many a mile
'Cross bog and hill and woodland too
Till the great mansion came in view.
'Stay here, my friend, I'll go alone,'
The ghost, upon the landing stone
Then gave the rapper such a knock,
McFadden shivered with the shock.
A window opened overhead,
The landlord's voice like thunder said:
'How dare you come here at midnight
And set my household in a fright?'
'Shove out the bolt, the night is thin,
And I will speak with you within.'
The window fell into its space,
And deathly quiet came o'er the place.
Then footsteps sounded in the hall –
It was the ghost, passed through the wall;
And up the stairs he then did glide:
The bedroom door flew open wide,
Ands as the ghost poked round his head
A pistol shot came from the bed.
The ghost gave out a scornful laugh:
'You might as well be throwing chaff.
Your shots have no effect on me,
I'm bullet-proof, as you may see.'
And as the ghost walked in the door,
The pistol fell upon the floor;
His hairs all stiff upon his head,
The landlord fainted in his bed.

The ghost then o'er the landlord bent:
'How dare you raise McFadden's rent?'
'Ah,' says the landlord, 'G'way from me,
I'll lave it as it used to be.'
'That will not do – it was too dear;
Charge him the half – five pound a year.'
The landlord scowled, but in his dread
He kept his wits and slyly said,
'The half, the half, and when you go,
I will instruct my agent so.'
'No,' said the ghost, 'That scheme won't do,
The pleas must now be signed, by you.'
To prove his point, he quickly then
Produced a paper, ink and pen.
'Five pound a year for McFadden's land'
Was written and signed with trembling hand.
The ghost then seized the document
And down the staircase quickly went.
He found McFadden at the door,
And handed him the paper o'er.
A sound cut short his thanks sincere
Which rang the world both far and near –
'Hear!' said the ghost. 'The cocks do crow!
Farewell, McFadden, I must go!

Nineteenth century, adapted from Mary Rogers,
Prospect of Fermanagh

Notes Boho in Fermanagh is a place where rites to Lugh were practised; 'Lawyer Dan' was Daniel McConnell.

183

The Death Coach

'Tis midnight! – how gloomy and dark!
By Jupiter, there's not a star –
'Tis fearful – 'tis awful – and hark!
What sound is that comes from afar?

Still rolling and rumbling, that sound
Makes nearer and nearer approach:
Do I tremble, or is it the ground?
Lord save us – what is it? A coach!

A coach! But that coach has no head;
And the horses are headless as it;
Of the driver the same may be said,
And the passengers inside who sit.

See the wheels! How they fly o'er the stones,
And whirl, as the whip it goes crack;
Their spokes are of dead men's thigh-bones,
And the pole is the spine of the back.

The hammer-cloth, shabby display,
Is a pall, rather mildew'd by damps;
And to light up the fearful array,
Two hollow skulls double as lamps.

From the gloom of Rathcooney churchyard
They dash down the hill of Glanmire;
Pass Lota in gallop as hard
As if these horses never could tire.

Though steep is the Tivoli lane,
Yet uphill to them is as down;
Not the charms of Woodhill do detain
Those Dullahans rushing to town.

And now it is past twelve o'clock;
Through the streets they rush on like the wind;
And, taking the road to Blackrock,
Cork City is soon left behind.

Up the Deadwoman's Hill they are rolled.
Boreenmannah is quite out of sight,
Ballintemple is reached, and behold!
At its graveyard they stop and alight.

'Who's there?' says a voice from the ground.
'No room here; the place is quite full.'
'Then room must be speedily found,
For us from the parish of Skull!

'Here for the night we'll lie down,
Tomorrow we speed on the gale;
For having no heads of our own –
We seek the Old Head of Kinsale!'

            T. C. Croker, from Fairy Legends
                        of the South of Ireland

Cormac and Mary

She is not dead – she has no grave –
She lives, beneath Lough Corrib's water;
And in the murmur of each wave,
Methinks I hear the songs I taught her.'

Thus many an evening on the shore
Sat Cormac, raving wild and lowly,
Still idly muttering o'er and o'er:
'She lives, detain'd by spells unholy.

'Death claims her not – too fair for earth,
Her spirit lives, afar from heaven;
Nor will it know a second birth
When sinful mortals are forgiven.

'Cold is this rock – the wind comes chill,
And gloomy mists the waters cover;
But oh! her soul is colder still,
To lose her God; to leave her lover!'

The lake was in profound repose,
Yet one white wave came gently curling,
And, as it reached the shore, arose
Dim figures, banners gray unfurling.

Onward they move, an airy crowd:
Through each thin form a moonlit ray shone,
While spear and helm, in pageant proud,
Appear in liquid undulation.

Bright barbed steeds curvetting tread
Their trackless way with antic capers,
And curtain-clouds hang overhead,
Festoon'd in rainbow-coloured vapours.

And when a breath of air would stir
That drapery of Heaven's own wreathing,
Light wings of filmy gossamer
Swayed and sparkled to that breathing.

Nor wanting was the choral song,
Swelling in silv'ry chimes of sweetness,
To sound of which this subtile throng
Advanced in playful grace and fleetness.

To music's strain, all came and went
Upon poor Cormac's doubting vision;
Now rising in wild merriment,
Now fading low in soft derision.

'Christ, save her soul!' he boldly cried;
And when that sacred name was spoken,
Fierce yells and fiendish shrieks replied,
And vanish'd all – the spell was broken.

And now on Corrib's lonely shore,
Freed by his word from powers of faery,
To life, to love, restored once more,
Young Cormac welcomes back his Mary.

> *T. C. Croker, from* Fairy Legends
> of the South of Ireland

Notes The following poem is a poetical rendering of
the story of Garrett Oge Fitzgerald, Eleventh Earl of
Kildare. At the pleading of his wife, he showed her
his magic powers, having first enjoined her not to
move or speak. But when he changed himself into a
bird and a black cat sprang at it, she could not resist
trying to stop it, and so broke the spell.

The Legend of Kilkea Castle

It is seven years since they last awoke
From their death-like sleep in Mullaghmast,
And the ghostly troop, with its snow-white horse,
On the Curragh plain in Kilkea rode past.
For the Lord of Kildare goes forth tonight,
And has left his rest in the lonely rath.
Oh, roughen the road for the silver shoes,
That they wear full soon on his homeward path.

So then to his own he may come again,
With a trumpet blast and his warriors bold,
And the spell that was by his lady cast,
Will pass away as a tale once told.
For dearly she loved her noble lord,
And she wished that no secret from her he kept,
So she begged to know why in chamber small
He watched and toiled while the household slept.

But the Wizard Earl would not tell to her
The secret dark of his vaulted cell,
'For fear,' he said, 'in the human frame
Lets loose the power of farthest Hell.'
But she feared for naught save his waning love,
And at length to her wish he bent an ear,
So flood, and serpent, and ghost gave place,
For the lady's heart had shown no fear.

Then her lord to a bird was soon transformed,
That rested its wing on her shoulder fair;
But the lady screamed and swooned away,
When a cat sprang forth from the empty air.
For a woman must fear for the one she loves,
And a woman's heart will break in twain,
When she knows that her hand had struck the blow,
To the man she had died to save from pain.

And thus the Earl must sleep as dead,
Till the silver shoes of his steed are worn,
By which, every seven years, they say,
To Kilkea and back to the rath he's borne.
And swiftly they pass, that phantom band,
With the Earl on his charger gleaming white,
So we think 'tis the shade of a cloud goes by,
With a shifting beam of the moon's pale light.

Peers Hervey

The Banshee of the MacCarthys

'Twas the Banshee's lonely wailing,
Well I knew that voice of death,
On the night wind slowly sailing
O'er the bleak and gloomy heath . . .
Who sits upon that heath forlorn,
With robe so free and tresses torn,
Anon she pours a harrowing strain,
And then she sits all mute again!
Now peals the wild funereal cry,
And now it sinks into a sigh.

T. C. Croker